Scent Talk
Among Animals

Scent Talk Among Animals

by Ruth Winter

Illustrated by Richard Cuffari

J. B. LIPPINCOTT COMPANY

PHILADELPHIA AND NEW YORK

U. S. Library of Congress Cataloging in Publication Data

Winter, Ruth, birth date
  Scent talk among animals.

  Bibliography: p.
  Includes index.
  SUMMARY: Discusses the scent language used by animals throughout the world for communication and behavior control.
  1. Smell—Juvenile literature. 2. Animals—Juvenile literature.
  [1. Smell. 2. Animals—Habits and behavior] I. Cuffari, Richard, birth date II. Title.
  QP458.W55   591.1′826   76-52935
  ISBN-O-397-31732-8

To Robin, Craig and Grant,
who always wondered about
the wonder of nature

The author wishes to thank the following who helped either directly or through their research reports:

Barry W. Ache, Lester Aronson, E. Ashare, William J. Bell, F. H. Bronson, T. W. Brooks, Kenneth Brown, Hilda M. Bruce, Albert Burgstahler, Theodore Burk, Doug Caroom, Mary Lou Cheal, L. G. Clemens, L. Coniglio, Jon Cooper, Madeline Cooper, Jane V. Davies, Richard G. Davis, Victor Denenberg, Marshall Devor, Michael Diamond, Richard L. Doty, Alison Fleming, Michael Fortuna, Robert Gandelman, Richard Gilluly, David M. Goldenberg, Arthur Goldfarb, Benjamin Hart, Arthur Hasler, Charles Haugen, Robert Heck, Robert I. Henkin, Bert Holldobler, Ross Horrall, Donald D. Jensen, R. B. Jones, Wolf A. Kafka, Howard Katz, James M. Kennedy, J. S. Kennedy, Bathsheva Kimelman, Gale Peter Largey, Richard A. Larson, John H. Law, Robert N. Leaton, Robert Lubow, D. Marsh, Michael Mattikow, Howard Moskowitz, D. J. Mulder, Michael Murphy, R. Mybytowgcz, R. D. Nadler, Walter Neuhaus, N. W. Nowell, Keith Owen, J. Bradley Powers, Hafeezur Rahaman, Katherine Ralls, Fred E. Regnier, Boyce Rensberger, Milo Richmond, Jay Rosenblatt, Manuel Salas, Gary Sams, Shawn Schapiro, Dietrich Schneider, E. Fred Schultz, Allan Scholz, Richard F. Seegal, Burton Slotnick, Richard L. Sprott, Robert A. Stehn, Bruce Svare, D. W. Swenson, Jack Tapp, Delbert D. Thiessen, Patricia Wallace, Edward A. Wasserman, David Rodney Watson, W. K. Whitten, Sarah S. Winanas.

Contents

I
What Smells?

Can sharks really smell a drop of blood in the ocean? Does a vulture sniff its prey from high in the sky? Do we smell bad to a skunk?

While you sit reading this book, all around you animals are conversing in a silent scent dialogue. A dog is sniffing a signpost for a message. A female moth is exuding a perfume to lure males from miles away. Ants are laying down scent trails and rabbits are building odor fences.

If you were to put down this book and take a walk in the woods, literally millions of creatures would smell you coming and dive into burrows or scamper up trees to get out of your way.

Each animal—including you and me—has a unique aroma composed not only of a species but also of a family and personal scent. In addition, all animals—with just a very few exceptions—have a sense of smell, and for most it is the most basic and useful sense.

Smell and taste are called the chemical senses because particles of odor and flavor substances must be dissolved in liquid to be recognized. That's why the nose and the mouth are bathed in fluids like mucus and saliva.

In some creatures, taste and smell receptors are so close together that scientists argue whether or not they are one combined sense, but in two highly developed forms of animal life—insects and vertebrates (those with backbones, including us)—the senses of smell and taste are clearly distinct. We smell with our noses and taste with our tongues. Bees smell with their antennae and taste with their mouth parts.

No matter how an animal does it, however, smell has an advantage over taste. Identifying something by taste requires direct contact, whereas things can be smelled from great distances. This gives the sense of smell an advantage over touch as well. In order to touch something, you have to be close to it. In a world where an enemy may quickly gobble you up when given a chance, it's better to keep safely away until you know for sure the other creature is friendly.

The sense of smell is also more useful than sight in most animals. The majority have poor eyesight and some are even born blind. Furthermore, sight is not very helpful in the dark or in thick foliage or in muddy waters. Two objects may look very much alike and often the only way to tell them apart is to smell them.

Sounds are hard to detect in a noisy environment. And if an animal uses audible signals to communicate with others of its kind, it may give away its exact location to enemies. Odors may not be so precise. Smells can permeate a wide area, day or night, and they have the added advantage of remaining to leave a message behind after an animal has gone.

But above all things, the chemical sense of smell (sometimes combined with taste) is needed by almost all animals to ensure proper nourishment. How else could a creature analyze foods—which are composed of chemicals—and determine which were good to eat?

Therefore, it is not surprising that the ability to smell is thought to have been the first sense to develop. There is a theory that when single cells floated around in the sea at the beginning of life on earth, it was a scent attractant that brought them together to form multicelled organisms. Whether this idea is correct or not, it's true that all smell cells—whether in the nose of a mouse or a man—are alike. Each of the cells has cilia—hairlike tissues—on the exposed side. On the inside there are nerve endings that lead directly to a part of the brain once called the rhinencephalon, meaning "nose brain."

Those animals which are great smellers—the macrosomatic, such as the bloodhound and the rabbit—have large brain areas which receive smell messages. Those animals which are lesser smellers—the microsomatic, such as humans and birds—have smaller brain smell areas. The whale and the dolphin, which are believed to have lost their sense of smell entirely, have almost no "nose brain" at all.

But even in creatures which are considered microsomatic, the sense of smell is still wonderfully powerful. We humans, for instance, can detect 0.000,000,000,000,071 of an ounce of skunk odor in the air.

Despite its importance, olfaction, the sense of smell, is the least understood of all the senses. No one is sure, for example, just how odor particles floating around in the air can be picked up by an animal's nose, transformed into electrical signals which are transmitted to the brain and then interpreted as "That smells like a rose" or "That's garbage."

Nevertheless, despite these mysteries, humans have always manipulated scents. The ancient Egyptians employed perfumes to send messages to the gods. The Chinese had a perfume clock with a different fragrance for each hour. The great African general, Hannibal, used his elephants not only to cross the Alps but to create a stink. He knew the stench of the huge beasts would send the enemy's horses into uncontrollable panic even before the armies met on the battlefield. Incidentally, elephants swing their trunks when walking to smell their way along. Their tiny eyes are not much good to them.

Skunks, of course, are even bigger stinkers than elephants. When those white-striped, bushy-tailed creatures let loose their scent, even their most ferocious opponents beat a hasty retreat.

Odor repellents and attractants in nature have long been observed by humans but the beginning of modern scientific study of smell messages probably began with the eighteenth-century naturalists. They were puzzled by the ability of virgin female moths to attract male moths from great distances, and they wondered if the females used a scent. Human noses could not detect any moth scent at all.

The critical experiment demonstrating that the attractant was, indeed, a self-made moth odor was described in 1879 by Jean Henri Fabre in his book, *Souvenirs Entomologiques.* The Frenchman wrote that when he picked up a female moth and put her under a glass hood, male moths that flew into his house through the open window ignored her and went, instead, to the spot where she had most recently been resting.

Other experimenters showed that male moths smelled the females with their antennae. When the antennae were removed or covered with varnish, the winged suitors were no longer interested in the come-hither perfume.

In the 1930s, a young German scientist with a lot of patience began slicing off the abdominal tips of 250,000 virgin female silk moths in an effort to extract the chemical lure. In 1959, twenty years and many chemical tests later, the scientist, Adolf F. J. Butenandt, and his co-

workers at the Max Planck Institute for Bio-
chemistry announced they had identified the
substance. They called it bombykol.

In order to extract twelve milligrams of pure
bombykol, the research team said, a biochemist
would need the glands of half a million moths.
But the substance was so powerful that if a
single female moth released all her perfume at
once, she could attract a billion males. If a
bathtub full of her chemical lure were mixed
into all the world's oceans, a teaspoonful of the
mixture would still attract moth suitors.

Since Butenandt and his colleagues isolated
bombykol, more than one hundred self-made
insect chemical lures have been identified and a
number of them have been reproduced artifi-
cially in the laboratory.

Meanwhile, it has been discovered in the past
two decades that insects use odor messages for
more purposes than just attracting mates. They
lay scent trails to direct their fellows to food,
send out odor alarms when an enemy is near,
use smell to identify the correct mate, odors to
control co-workers and, in fact, have an amaz-
ingly versatile scent vocabulary. Furthermore,
within the past few years, it has been observed

that not only insects but most mammals, including humans, also send out scent messages.

In 1959, scent messages were given a formal name—pheromones—from the Greek *pherein* meaning "to carry" and *horman* meaning "to excite, to stimulate." Unlike hormones, the powerful products of ductless glands, which are secreted into the bloodstream to affect an animal's own development, reproduction and behavior, pheromones are secreted externally and exert a specific effect at a distance on the behavior and body of another of the same species.

We are just now beginning to understand animals' scent talk.

II
Something Smells Fishy

The horror tales are quite similar. A sailor is shipwrecked and floundering in the sea or a swimmer is happily paddling around in the ocean waves and suddenly, without warning, a huge, multi-toothed, torpedolike creature attacks. The frail human body is usually no match for the massive jaws of the monster.

How did the shark know a human was in the water? Why did it attack?

Sharks appeared in pretty much the same shape they are today more than 400 million years ago. They were the first successful group of sea swimmers and they have been living death machines ever since.

There are 350 species of sharks, ranging from six inches to sixty feet in size and from a few ounces to five tons in weight. Most are harmless to humans. There are only about twelve deaths from shark attacks each year, far fewer than the fatalities caused by allergic reactions to insect stings.

All shark species lack bones. They are essentially a mass of cartilage covered by a tough hide which scrapes like a thousand sharp razor blades. They ingest everything from broken bottles to one-hundred-pound sea lions.

Sharks are stupid. You could hold the brain of a twenty-foot killer white in the palm of your hand. But the area of that brain used for smell messages would be about two-thirds of the brain's entire weight. The shark's super weapon, therefore, is not its teeth but its sense of smell. It can detect one part of blood in 100 million parts of water. Shark hunters know that if they toss chum, a slick of blood and fish oils that stays on the surface of the water, sharks from miles around will gather at the spot within minutes.

Under ordinary circumstances, however, sharks don't come near surface waters by the shore during the day. They swim at night when few humans are likely to be within reach of their jaws.

Wounded, sick or crazy sharks are different. They may make an appearance at any time. Furthermore, humans wearing diving equipment have more and more invaded the normal habitat of these monsters of the deep.

Sharks are attracted by the smell of blood. Their characteristic weaving motion while swimming is due to their sniffing for scent molecules, first with one nostril and then with the other, as they attempt to follow the odor trail. As the shark draws nearer to the prey, its other senses help direct it. It has special fluid-filled canals which pick up vibrations. That's

Great White Shark

why the erratic swimming motions of a human are felt, by the shark, to be the floundering of a wounded fish.

About fifty yards from the target, the color-blind shark will sight its prey. It then circles several times to obtain a good look before striking. Sensory cells along its snout, which are believed to pick up minute changes in electrical charge, guide it in to the target, much like radar guides a plane. The shark has completed a

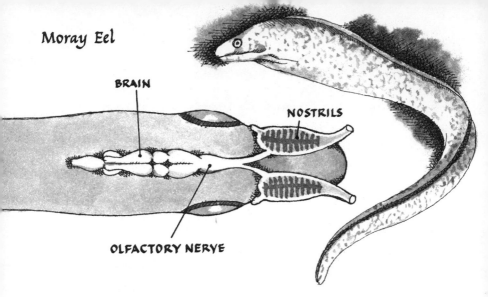

Moray Eel

BRAIN

NOSTRILS

OLFACTORY NERVE

journey begun miles away when its long-distance receptor, smell, picked up the scent of blood or another attractive chemical.

Another supersmeller of the deep is the moray eel, which breeds in the Atlantic waters of North America, Europe and the Mediterranean. The moray's ability to detect and follow odors is supposedly many times better than that of the earthbound bloodhound.

Female eels grow to about four feet in length and males to about two feet. Their teeth, located in the heads of their narrow, snakelike bodies, are almost as evil-looking as those of the shark.

Morays love to eat small octopuses, but the

eel's favorite food has a special defensive weapon. When attacked or pursued by the super-smelling eel, the dome-headed, eight-legged octopus releases a cloud of black "ink" which acts as a smoke screen and numbs the eel's sense of smell.

Oceanographers have watched as an eel passes up a juicy octopus, even with direct contact, because the ink had shut off the moray's sense of smell.

Another member of the mollusk family, the arrow-headed, ten-footed squid, also uses smell power. French and Swiss researchers discovered that the embryonic squid does not wriggle out of its egg prematurely because the fluid inside the egg contains a natural tranquilizer. The experimenters extracted this substance, mixed it with water and released it near vigorously swimming squid which had already hatched. Within an instant, the young squid became inactive. The squid-calming scent had the same effect on small crustaceans such as shrimp and on some kinds of young fish.

Many fish have a very efficient scent alarm system which works well in water, although it has its disadvantages. It can't be released until one of the fish is injured or dead.

This was dramatically demonstrated when an

experimenter took a fish from a nearby stream, grazed its skin slightly and put the fish into a jam jar filled with water. After a few minutes, he poured the water from the jar into the stream. A school of fish began taking big gulps of water and then, as if an electric shock had occurred, the fish began to panic and flee. For several days afterward, the disturbed fish rejected food.

So far, shock substances have been found only in one order of fish, Ostariophysi. However, this order is a large one. Among its five thousand species are two-thirds of all freshwater fish, including trout, graylings and white fish, and many saltwater fish such as sardines and herrings. Tadpoles, fishlike frog babies, also have a shock chemical. The tadpoles' shock chemical does not seem to affect fish but the carp's warning signal puts crustaceans such as lobsters to quick flight and slowly affects the fright reaction of salmon. Many of these shock chemicals work in both fresh and salt water.

The sea anemone, a creature with a stalklike body topped by a ring of tentacles, cannot easily flee but it, too, makes use of alarm chemicals. The anemone draws in its tentacles to its base when frightened much as we put our hands over our heads to protect ourselves from danger. When an anemone upstream is injured, within seconds the anemones downstream show this alarm reaction.

Investigators who have chemically analyzed the sea anemone's alarm substance found it to be very similar to our detergent compounds. However, little is really known about the structure of most fish shock substances. Scientists believe that such compounds are far less specific than insect pheromones because fish shock chemicals affect more than one kind of fish while insect alarm scents affect only members of a single species.

Perhaps the fish shock substance most carefully studied is that of minnows, those tiny stream swimmers.

Minnows are not very good parents. They like to eat their own children. They evidently lack the inhibition of most animal mothers and fathers. Without a means of protecting the youngsters, the species would self-destruct.

As a group of scientists watched, a school of young minnow fry were peacefully paddling around. A large adult minnow suddenly swam up. The fry did not flee because they weren't mature enough to react to the danger. The adult minnow eagerly gobbled up a little fish and still the other youngsters swam around unconcerned. The big cannibal, however, suddenly panicked and fled.

What had happened? The observers believe that when the big minnow tore up the little one with its mouth, a shock substance was released from the youngster's skin. As soon as the adult fish smelled this chemical, it became alarmed and fled. The young minnows remained unimpressed because their sensitivity to the shock substance had not yet matured. They develop a reaction to it at about four to eight weeks of age.

In order for the alarm chemical to work, however, one little minnow has to die for the sake of the others.

Minnows use their sense of smell not only to identify the shock substance but to recognize their traditional enemy, the pike. When the small defenseless minnows catch an approaching pike's odor, they do not attempt to flee. The pike is much faster and could catch them. Instead, the little fish become totally immobile and sink to the bottom of the water. The pike, which is primarily sight-guided, reacts chiefly to the sight of motion, and so it passes by the minnows.

Mussels, snails and clams, on the other hand,

try to dig in and hide when they smell their great enemy, the starfish, approaching. Sometimes, hiding is to no avail. The five-armed predator will creep slowly along the ocean floor and then suddenly twitch and return to a spot it has just passed. It will dig a hole about two feet in diameter and four inches deep and, within a few seconds, pull out a hapless clam or mussel. The starfish can smell its prey through four inches of sand.

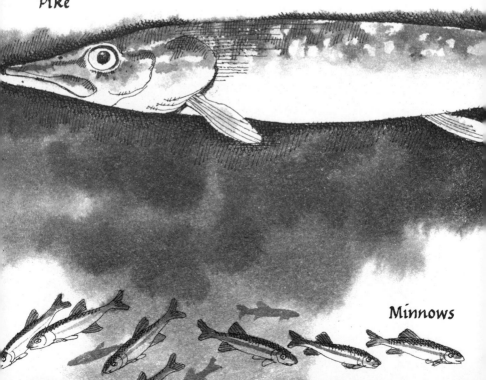

Pike

Minnows

Like the starfish, many creatures which live in water use smell—perhaps combined with taste—to find food, to locate a mate, to identify enemies, to join schools and to return home. Vision is usually limited in water and some fish are totally blind.

Fish do use touch, which is located all over their skin. In fact, it is said that if we had their same tactile ability, we would be able to touch a chair and know which of our friends had last sat in it during the day.

On land, odorants are mostly airborne, but in water they are dissolved. Therefore, there is an argument among scientists as to whether or not smell and taste can be considered separate senses in creatures that live in water, since they both involve the recognition of dissolved substances. The taste and smell receptors, however, do differ anatomically in fish as they do in higher vertebrates. Fish evidently smell with their noses and taste with their mouths. Most researchers think that the fishes' sense of smell, not their sense of taste, is keener. It is their most important means of receiving information from their surroundings. They can detect an odor if it has been diluted in an ocean of water.

Catfish, for instance, are nearly blind. They

are supersmellers like the shark but they are far more intelligent. These bewhiskered swimmers use odors to regulate most of their social behavior.

A bullhead catfish can immediately detect the water in which a recent opponent has been swimming and he can recognize each member of his school by scent.

The members of the school, on the other hand, can smell defeat. When a normally dominant boss catfish is bested in a fight or is beginning to lose his strength, the other fish know it before he does. His odor is altered.

Catfish also possess a tranquilizing substance similar to the one produced for the benefit of squid embryos. The catfish use it to calm crowds.

Experimenters discovered that when they dumped water from an overcrowded tank into a tank containing just a few feisty catfish, the active fish suddenly calmed down.

The theory is that the tranquilizer allows a large school to live peacefully together. It is possible that this calming pheromone could be employed by fish farmers to conserve large fish populations.

Since the catfish is so good at smelling and at

producing smells, Dr. Vernon A. Benignus, a psychologist at Trinity University, San Antonio, Texas, used them for experimental subjects. He placed electrodes in the smell areas of their brains so he could record their brains' electrical response to odors.

Dr. Benignus found that the catfishes' brains showed a strong reaction to a chemical, morphylene, which smells like dirty socks, and to ethyl mercaptan, which stinks of rotten eggs. But more surprising than that, catfish loved the smell of saltwater shrimp. Since the catfish used by Dr. Benignus were a freshwater species and had presumably never smelled brine shrimp before, the researcher decided to check his findings. He used shrimp as bait and fished for catfish. The bait was sensational. The catfish gobbled it up, hook and all.

Why freshwater catfish like shrimp is a mystery, but one thing is certain: they are adversely affected by pollution. Researchers found that detergents in water make the fish unable to smell and consequently unable to find food. In order to survive, a catfish and other water creatures must possess an ability to discriminate between odors. They have to be able to distinguish between what is food and what is not.

Lobsters, too, it has been found, stop eating for a long time when nonfatal levels of pollutants such as kerosene are placed in their tank. The eight-legged, two-pinchered lobsters are dull of sight. They have, instead, a powerful olfactory sense which is excited by scum and other ordinarily unappetizing ocean garbage.

Crabs, like lobsters, like decaying flesh for food. It is believed that crabs and other crustaceans taste with their feet and smell with their antennae. Experimenters put a dead squid into a crab's tank and watched as the crab scraped the bottom with its claws and lifted the claws to its mouth. The crab then walked around the tank until it made contact with the dead squid, took it into its claws, tore off small pieces and ate them.

The researchers then took an extract of dead squid and soaked a piece of filter paper in it. Then they placed the filter paper in the tank. Sure enough, the crab put the paper in its mouth, but when ordinary, untreated filter paper was put into the tank, the crab ignored it.

Crayfish, small, lobsterlike freshwater crustaceans, also show odor-influenced behavior. The males are very aggressive when confronted with other males but are well-behaved in the presence of females.

Crayfish courtship always begins with threatening behavior on the part of both male and female but the battle soon turns into a series of peaceful movements. The change is believed to be the result of a tranquilizing pheromone released by the female.

Scientists tested this theory by placing an opaque container in the tank of a male crayfish. The unit had holes in it so that water could pass through it, but the crayfish in the tank could not see the one in the container. When the mystery crayfish in the container was a male, the crayfish in the tank took an aggressive stance. But when it was a female, the crayfish performed courtship movements and acted as if he were offering food to a mate.

Behavior control by sex pheromones is believed to be widespread among fish, although this has been demonstrated for just a few species. With some kinds of fish, at least, it has been observed that a female's scent calms an aggressive male fish and a male's scent makes a female fish stop swimming so he can mate with her.

In the case of sea urchins, odors permit sex by remote control. The entire sex life of the male and female of these sea porcupines consists of

ejecting the sperm and the egg into the seawa-
ter. The spermatozoids then swim about and
fertilize whatever eggs they happen to meet.
This method is too haphazard for survival in a
big ocean, unless the ejection of sperms and
eggs is timed correctly. The urchins communicate by releasing an odor substance into the
water along with the eggs or sperm. This chemical acts as a signal to any urchin of the opposite
sex which happens to be in the area to follow
suit.

Other aquatic creatures have a chemical
means of birth control. Scientists observed that
when large tadpoles, fishlike baby frogs, are
placed in a tank with smaller tadpoles, the
younger ones are overcome by a fatal loss of
appetite. Even when offered abundant food, the
youngsters stop feeding and soon die. They act
the same way when only the water from the tank
of the bigger tadpoles is poured into theirs. It is
believed that the younger tadpoles stop eating
because of a smell signal released by the older
ones. Thus, overcrowding is prevented, and the
older tadpoles have a better chance of surviving
to maturity.

As amazing as this phenomenon may be, there
is nothing more spectacular when it comes to

Chinook Salmon

smell language among fish than the salmon migration which has fascinated fishermen and scientists for years.

Sometime between eighteen months and seven years after they hatch, depending upon the species, the river-born fish, which have matured in the ocean, are now ready to return to the place of their birth. They gather at a depression near the mouth of the stream, and peacefully loll around while awaiting the gathering of their companions.

At a certain time, probably signaled by scent, they begin their run upstream. No obstacle can stop them. They engage in a grueling race against death which covers hundreds of miles and progresses at an average speed of two and a half miles per hour. They swim without feeding, day and night, reaching their goal within two or three weeks.

If they pick up the scent of a predator, for instance a fisherman or a bear standing in the water, the fish make an attempt to skirt the source of the smell.

The enormous effort of the race upstream consumes 96 percent of their body fat and 53 percent of their protein. Their feeding and digestive organs shrivel while their sex organs grow large.

The salmon lose their silvery sheen and turn first dirty yellow and then olive green. The males' mouths lengthen and curve into the shape of a pair of pliers and an ugly, inedible hump rises on their backs. Their gill plates become hard and brittle and their ability to breathe becomes less and less.

Despite their deteriorating physical condition, the male salmon fight one another fiercely as soon as they reach the spawning grounds. The females, in the meantime, dig hollows about ten inches deep in the calmer stretches of the riverbed and deposit about two thousand eggs each. The victors of the male battles then fertilize the eggs. Because only the fittest males contribute to the gene pool, the young are more likely to be strong enough to make the run. Soon after they spawn, both parents die.

This spectacular migration had long been described but scientists wondered whether the salmon were actually returning to the place where they were born to spawn and die. How could they possibly remember it after so long in the sea?

In 1939, Dr. W. A. Clemens, a Canadian researcher, carried out an experiment. In a tributary of the Fraser River System, he tagged 469,326 young salmon heading for the Pacific. Years later, he caught 10,958 returning salmon with his mark. The most astonishing thing was that no other tributary of the Fraser had any of the marked salmon.

The fish, therefore, had not simply swum from the sea into just any river and from there into just any tributary to spawn. The terrible trial of their last days was to reach the place where they, themselves, had been born.

What is it that makes the salmon go back to

their homes to breed—and to die without reproducing if conditions are not just right? How do the fish find their way home?

Professor Arthur D. Hasler of the University of Wisconsin caught returning salmon from two arms of a river in the state of Washington. He transported them downstream again, below the river's fork. He blocked the nostrils of half the fish he had caught. Then he released all the salmon. The fish with the unblocked nostrils all chose the tributary into which they had swum the first time. The fish who had lost their sense of smell also lost their bearings. They swam first one way and then the other, unable to make a definite choice between the two arms of the river.

There is little doubt now that salmon do, indeed, follow their noses. The scent of home is indelibly marked in their brains. Another University of Wisconsin scientist, Dr. Allan T. Sholz, and his colleagues in the department of zoology confirmed this in a report in the June 1976 issue of *Science.* They described how young salmon were exposed to either morpholine or to phenethyl alcohol for one and a half months and then released into Lake Michigan. Eighteen months later, when this species of salmon were ready for their spawning migration, morpholine was put into one stream and phenethyl alcohol into another. The scientists watched as those fish exposed to the dirty-sock smell of morpholine swam directly toward the morpholine stream while those which had been exposed to alcohol returned to the alcohol-treated stream. This demonstrated to the researchers that salmon remember and utilize chemical cues in their spectacular return to their birthplace.

Although there is much yet to learn about fish pheromones, it is already clear that sensitivity to chemicals in water plays the same role as sensitivity to chemicals in air does for land animals. It controls attraction to food, recognition of predators, social and mating behavior and migration.

It is easy to see, therefore, how fish behavior can be disrupted by chemical pollution.

III
Reptiles, Amphibians and Sea Mammals

Remember those early jungle pictures where a crocodile would slither into the water from the riverbank, its toothy jaws wide open in pursuit of Tarzan or some hapless native peacefully bathing?

Well, the crocodile didn't have its mouth open in order to eat Tarzan or the native—it was trying to find them. The eyes of the large, long-snouted reptile are not much good. They are set far back on its head. Therefore, the crocodile must rely heavily on scent, and its smell receptors are located in its throat.

Crocodilians first made an appearance on earth about 175 million years ago. They have heavy, cylindrical bodies, a large triangular head, short legs and a strong, flat tail.

The largest crocodile on record was twenty-three feet long. Most are between twelve and fifteen feet.

All modern crocodilians, with the exception of the American and Chinese alligators, reside in the tropics or subtropics. All are amphibious by habit, living in and along lakes, marshes and rivers.

Crocodiles frequently float on the surface of the water with only the tip of their snouts and their eyes atop their head projecting. Their nostrils, which are at the tip of their snouts, are surrounded by muscles that can contract to prevent water from entering. Their ears can also be closed off by muscles to prevent flooding.

The big beasts have no lips. Their skins are directly attached to their skulls without muscular padding so that water constantly seeps into their mouths. Large muscular flaps that close off the back of their mouths keep them from drowning.

When crocodiles submerge, they leave their nostrils out of the water so that they can breathe and receive odor messages which are

directed to the back of their throats. If they catch a whiff of something significant, they open their jaws to get a better smell.

When a crocodile sees or smells an approaching animal, bird or fish, it opens its mouth, seizes the prey with its jaws and drowns it. If the meal is too large to swallow at once, then the crocodile tears it into pieces and eats it.

Like all but a few reptiles, the crocodile has no sound-producing mechanism, and, like most reptiles, it has very poor hearing. The lizardlike tuatara of New Zealand grunts and some sea turtles reportedly scream when angry, but generally, reptiles communicate by vision and by smell.

Crocodiles produce self-made odor messages. The bull alligator, for instance, uses a scent produced by glands under its lower jaw to attract a mate. The putrid odor hangs over the swamps like a fog. Female alligators love it.

Another reptile which uses odors to communicate is the turtle. The female emits a stink similar to the male alligator's to inform potential mates of her readiness to be courted. Male turtles, in turn, produce their own stinking chemical to warn off other males who might be rivals for the same female.

Turtles are about as old as the crocodiles.

While reptiles like the dinosaurs flourished and vanished and others like the snakes and lizards persisted and evolved, the good, slow turtle plodded along through evolution, changing very little en route.

Probably their protective shells enabled them to survive, despite the fact that they have been toothless since they first appeared on earth more than 150 million years ago. In some types, the horny jaws function as teeth, but generally food is clasped by the turtle's forelimbs, mashed and then put in the mouth and mashed some more before swallowing.

Turtles range from the size and weight of a nickle to a seven-foot-long, shelled monster weighing a ton. No matter how large or small, turtles all seem to rely heavily on the sense of smell. They are able to distinguish colors and to pick up strong vibrations, but they cannot hear sounds very well.

One aspect of turtle behavior has intrigued humans for a long time. Female sea turtles leave the water, dig a hole in the sand and lay eggs. They cover the eggs with sand and in about sixty days, warmed by the sun, the eggs hatch. As soon as the baby turtles emerge from the eggs, they know the most direct way to the sea. How? Perhaps it is the difference in light between land and sea or perhaps it is the smell of the water. No one knows for sure.

There was one mystery which a turtle helped solve.

American snapping turtles are called "dogs of the inland lakes" because of their ability to track scents. In the 1920s, there was a series of murders which made headlines. A fiend in the Midwest taunted police by reporting each time he killed a victim; the law officers could not find the bodies.

Through informants and other leads, the police learned that the murderer put the bodies into sacks, weighted them with heavy stones and sank the sacks into deep lakes. The police were stymied because they couldn't find the corpses, and without the bodies they couldn't prove there had been murders.

An elderly Indian appeared at police headquarters one day and volunteered to locate the bodies. He had one rule, however: No one could watch him do it. Sure enough, the next day the Indian pointed to a spot in one of the lakes and said there was a corpse below. There was.

The Indian repeated his feat several times. Law officers could stand their curiosity no longer. They followed him and watched as the old Indian placed a huge snapping turtle attached

to a string over the side of his boat. It took the Indian only a few hours to find the spot where a body lay. He knew that the bloodhound-like snapping turtle delighted in the taste of decayed flesh. If there was a corpse in the water, the reptile's nose would soon lead him to it. When the string attached to the turtle stopped moving and remained taut, the Indian knew that the turtle had found the body.

Unlike turtles, snakes have frightened humans since the beginning of time. Not without reason. An estimated thirty thousand people die each year from their poisonous bites. Of course, only a few snakes are poisonous and some are even beneficial to humans.

Snakes are scaly, limbless, stretched-out creatures. The smallest, the thread snake, is about the size of a piece of spaghetti. The largest, the python, can exceed thirty feet in length.

Snakes, even more than crocodiles and turtles, rely almost entirely on their sense of smell to locate food. When a snake darts its tongue in and out of its head, it is not preparing to strike, it is picking up information from the environment. Its sense of smell is located in its nose and in the roof of its mouth.

Snakes and lizards have no direct connection between the nasal cavity and the roof of the mouth as most humans do. The opening has been closed and replaced by a cavity containing a nerve that leads directly to the brain's smell center. The cavity with this receiver is called Jacobson's organ.

If a strong odor or vibration stimulates a snake, its tongue flicks in and out rapidly to pick up odor particles. The forked tip with any odorants adhering to it is then rubbed against the opening of Jacobson's organ in the roof of the mouth. In effect, Jacobson's organ is a supplement to taste—it's a short-range chemical receptor in contrast to the long-range receptors of the true sense of smell located in the nasal tubes.

A number of humans also have Jacobson's organ. It forms in the third month of gestation near the front of the lower part of the nose. There is a slight opening in a short blind tube which runs upward and backward. Some people never lose it and doctors, during an operation, will notice this vestigal remnant of Jacobson's organ in humans.

Snakes, particularly pit vipers, also have heat sensors in their heads. These temperature receptors are used to locate warm-blooded prey at night, when eyes aren't very useful and smell may not give exact enough information to strike accurately.

There is much that is unknown about snake pheromones but we know that at least some species produce scent signals. Garter snakes are reported to smell musky when scared and an angry rattler is said to smell like a cut-open green watermelon.

Scientists believe most snakes attract mates by dancing and other movements, rather than by odor, but certain snakes are completely blind and prairie rattlesnakes have been observed coming from great distances to mass together, probably because of some scent signal.

Snakes and other reptiles are cold-blooded,

lung-breathing animals which first appeared later than amphibians and before birds or mammals.

Amphibians are also cold-blooded. These peculiar creatures were the first with backbones to leave their watery homes for land—some 335 million years ago. Only three groups of them exist today—the frogs and toads, the salamanders and the nearly blind, wormlike caecilians of the tropics. As their name implies, most amphibians spend part of their time on land and part in the water.

All mature amphibians have legs, lungs and nostrils. Their sense organs can operate both in air and water. Salamanders are believed to have the best sense of smell among amphibians. The caecilians have tentacles on either side of their snout which serve as both feelers and organs of smell. Both salamanders and caecilians have a poor sense of hearing, while the frog has an excellent one.

The first vertebrates to have voice boxes were amphibians. When a frog croaks, air is expelled from its lungs, passes over the vocal cords and enters the mouth. The frog's good sense of hearing enables it to receive sound signals.

Unlike reptiles, which do not have to return

to water to breed, amphibians lay soft eggs in the form of spawn which floats on the water. The spawn develops into free-swimming larvae called tadpoles, newtpoles and toadpoles.

Tadpoles, as described in the chapter on fish, respond to odors. When small ones are placed in a tank with larger ones, the smaller tadpoles stop eating and die.

Although there is little information about mature amphibians' use of odors, they all apparently have a scent language.

The strong odor of ponds and sluggish streams has been found to attract frogs to their breeding grounds. On a number of occasions, researchers have observed frogs traveling long distances over land to a specific body of water. The frogs have floated down creeks for several miles, emerged from the water, climbed over a steep hill and continued overland until they reached the breeding pond.

Many amphibians secrete defensive chemicals from head glands. The Colorado toad squirts a poison from a pocket behind its eye for distances up to twelve feet. So effective is this weapon that dogs are said never to attack Colorados twice. On the other hand, the common toothless toad, tree frogs and many other amphibians secrete a harmless but very pungent smell substance that makes them unattractive to potential predators.

A species of salamander, meanwhile, uses a scent secreted from a special gland on its head to lure a mate. The male faces the female, flips his tail over his head and thrashes it about vigorously. The thrashing creates a water current which carries his scent to the female.

Another group of creatures which can live on either land or water consists of snails, also called gastropods or stomach walkers.

Snails are the largest mollusk class and among the most widely distributed of all groups of animals. Among mollusks, a group which includes octopuses and clams, they are the only ones to adapt to life on land. The majority of snails, however, live in brackish marine or freshwater habitats. They are found in the depths of the oceans and on the tops of high mountains, in deserts and in lakes.

Like the turtle, most snails carry their homes on their backs. One type, the cone shell or Conus, is not harmful to man if handled gently, but if handled carelessly, its dartlike teeth can inject a fatal poison.

Snails feed in a variety of ways on many kinds

of food. Some orders eat meat and others eat vegetation. Some have a ribbonlike tongue which they flick out; it works like a conveyor belt, carrying food back into the mouth. Many have horny jaws which cut off small particles of food. Some use mucus traps to snare food as it passes by.

Little is known about most snails' sense of smell, although the marine snail, the Nassarius, certainly seems to possess a good one. A dead fish in the water will attract Nassarius from relatively long distances. They gather in large numbers to feed on it.

With at least two of the marine species, the Hailotis and the Patella, the eggs and sperm are shed into the water and fertilization is external. Since sea urchins, which breed in the same manner, use scent signals for remote control of fertilization, presumably these snails do also.

While reptiles live mostly on land and amphibians live both on land and in water, seals and walruses returned to the water after having once lived on land. They still have fur, like earthbound mammals, but they are much more gregarious than most land mammals. They live in colonies called rookeries whose members may number up to a million.

Seals and walruses have a well-developed sense of smell and it is presumed that parents and children identify each other in the massive crowds by scent.

Sea mammals such as the whales and dolphins, on the other hand, have little or no sense of smell. Their olfactory nerves are vestigial like our appendix and the smell areas of their brains are apparently nonexistent. Whales and dolphins may have a good sense of taste, but no one is quite sure.

There is still much to be learned about the anatomy and behavior of reptiles, amphibians and sea mammals. We know very little about how they converse with scents, although it seems that, with a few exceptions, they all do.

IV
Insects—
The Supersmellers

Termites are among the most social of the social insects. As a matter of fact, they believe in equality of the sexes. In other social insect groups there is a single queen and males perform no function except mating, but termites have a king and queen that marry for life and both sexes work in all job categories.

Often mistaken for white ants, termites are very ancient. They probably appeared shortly after the cockroach, 200 to 300 million years ago. We humans have been here for only 1.5 million years and may be long gone before the termites vanish. Maybe that's because no one ever heard of a solitary termite. They all live in cooperative colonies that sometimes include millions of members.

There are an estimated two thousand different species of termites, most of them tropical. Only two species live in Europe and fifty-five in North America.

The North American species do not build large mounds as tropical termites do. Instead, they live in wood and cause considerable damage—reportedly equal to that caused by fire—each year. They tunnel through fence posts, wooden buildings, trees, wooden bridges and other structures. In homes, they eat cloth, books and paper.

The United States has three types of termites. The subterranean, the smallest and most destructive, nest underground and under wooden structures. The damp-wood termites live only in very moist wood and are primarily a Pacific Coast problem. The dry-wood termites, which need little moisture, are bothersome in the Southwest.

When a termite colony becomes too crowded, a smell level is probably reached which signals a special female to leave home and fly through the air. After she descends to the ground, she breaks off her wings along a sort of dotted line near the base and secretes a short-range come-hither perfume. The future queen then raises the tip of her abdomen and wiggles. Any male termite who happens to be passing is immediately attracted.

The male and the female begin a courtship dance, snuggling up to each other as they parade around, looking for a crevice or a timber in which to set up housekeeping. When they find the right spot, they construct a royal bed chamber, a "copularium."

Married for life, the king and queen mate periodically. She may lay eight thousand eggs per day and she becomes immobilized by her gigantic and continual pregnancies. Her abdomen elongates to about four inches. She is completely dependent upon her mate for everything and she keeps him in attendance by secreting a pheromone. In fact, experimenters who have broken open termite nests have been impressed by the king's reluctance to leave his mate, despite the danger to his own life.

When a king or queen dies, one or more young termites may develop into unwinged secondary reproductives to substitute for the lost royal mate.

The king and queen nourish their first offspring themselves, but after that, they stick strictly to their task of reproduction and leave the nursing to others.

The colony slowly grows in size, and at maturity, it is capable of producing all castes, a capability it may retain for many years before decline sets in, leading to ultimate destruction.

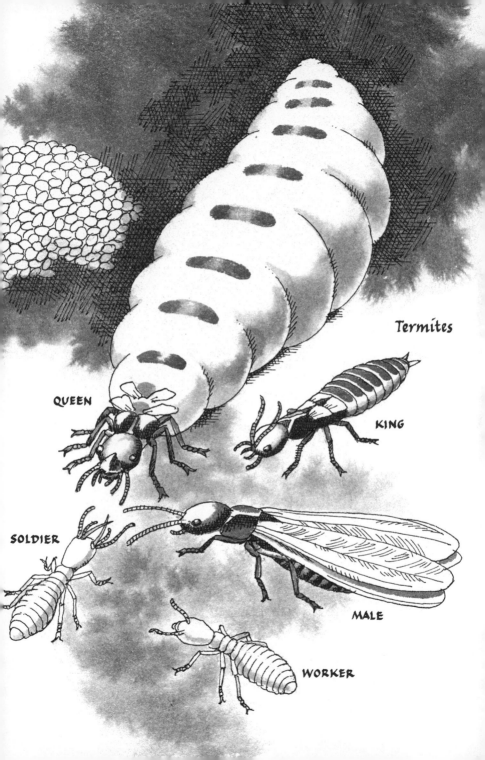

QUEEN

KING

Termites

SOLDIER

MALE

WORKER

Scent messages, pheromones, play a crucial role in maintaining caste balance within a termite society. Most of the first offspring become workers, although a few, perhaps 10 percent, become soldiers.

The workers are immature forms called nymphs. They are the most numerous members of a colony. They have a lot of work to do. They enlarge the galleries, feed the king and queen, carry the eggs away from the queen and nourish younger nymphs that are not yet able to eat by themselves.

Pheromones tell the workers who's who. Scents set them to grooming and to exchanging nutrients and to providing the secretions necessary to colony life.

Selective cannibalism occurs in termite societies during times of food shortages. It also occurs when there is a need to dispose of injured or surplus members of a caste. The process generally appears to begin with frantic grooming, probably causing a leakage of body fluid which creates a "funeral" scent. This scent triggers behavior in which the termites either eat "the dead" or construct special cemeteries within the mound in which to bury their murdered co-workers.

The existence of a special colony odor, even within a given species, has been demonstrated by scientists. When experimenters mixed termites from two colonies, the insects dueled to the death. The special colony scents are obviously important to cohesion. They consist of an aroma of body, food and environmental components. When a colony is divided in two, the odor of each section slowly changes. After a period of about three months, the smells are sufficiently distinct to cause fighting when the two halves are reunited.

Almost all termite colonies possess soldiers for defense. Soldiers have no wings, no eyes and much-reduced reproductive organs. Adult soldiers serve only for defense and are incapable of feeding themselves. Workers must shove food into their mouths.

Soldiers of most termite colonies have enlarged heads and jaws but there are some who have reduced jaws. Instead, the front of their heads is shaped into a "squirt gun" which forcibly ejects a sticky, irritating liquid into the eyes and mouths of the enemy. This weapon is particularly effective against marauding ants.

When a colony is in danger of attack, the termite soldiers all do a shiver and shake and emit an alarm scent. This serves to alert the entire colony quickly to the presence of danger. Reinforcements are drawn to the site of attack.

When they are not fighting, termite soldiers secrete a special smell which has a profound effect on the development of the colony young. The scent keeps the nymphs' growth glands from enlarging, which in turn keeps them small and modest workers. But if the army has suffered heavy losses during battle, there is insufficient soldier odor to prevent the nymphs' growth, and many develop into giant fighters to fill in the ranks.

There is still much that is unknown about these ancient insects but there is more information about them than about most other insects, with the exception of ants and bees.

There are an estimated 2 million species of insects, 80 percent of all known animal life on earth. Most insects are less than a quarter inch long. They live on and in every land and freshwater habitat. They come in infinite varieties. There are more species of flies in France, for instance, than there are of mammals in the whole world.

Not all insects are harmful to man. They help to pollinate plants. Many are part of the food chains on which our life depends and some are used to provide useful products such as dyes, silks and shellac. Some are just beautiful to behold like the Monarch butterfly.

There are about ten thousand species which are harmful to man either because they carry disease directly to him or because they destroy food and products. The cockroach, for instance, may carry typhoid and cholera and the mosquito can infect humans with encephalitis and yellow fever. The corn borer destroys corn crops and the boll weevil damages cotton. The larvae of certain moths destroy wool, and bookworms eat books.

We humans have never been completely successful in our battle against bugs. Maybe one reason is because there are so many. There are at least 4 million insects per moist acre of land, the majority of which are never observed.

For rare insects such as the dragonfly sight is the primary sense but for most insects smell is by far the most important. Organs of smell are usually thin hairs or tiny cones situated either on the antennae or in the mouth.

The sense of smell is so acute in most insects, and so effective over long distances, that researchers often find it mind-boggling.

Scientists have been aware of information exchange among the insects for a long time. More than two thousand years ago, the great Greek thinker Aristotle sat and pondered about the honey bee. He observed that even though a source of food placed near a hive might remain undiscovered for days, once one bee found it, all the others soon came around. Aristotle wanted to know how the message was delivered from one bee to the others. He found that even if the discoverer bee was captured on its way back to the hive, it still somehow delivered the news to its companions.

In 1920, one of the great zoologists of all time, Karl von Frisch, partially revealed the secrets of honey bee communication. He set two plates containing various scented foods near a hive. He found that after one bee had discovered a dish of food, the other bees approached only the dish from which the discoverer had fed.

By painstaking observation, von Frisch found that the first bee would return to the hive and do a circular dance. The faster the dance, the closer the source of food was to the hive. The bee would use the angle of the sun to give exact directions.

Later researchers observed that other bees

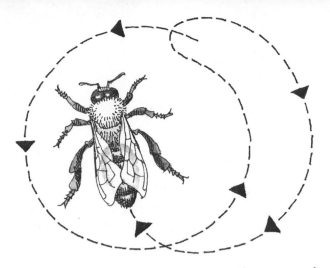

Bee Round Dance

would use their antennae to smell the pollen on the belly of the first bee. The smell would tell them exactly what kind of food had been found.

The discoverer bee, therefore, could tell its hive mates that there was clover a half mile away, 30 degrees south of the sun.

Other scientists have found that honey bees can relay messages either by a dance or by an odor or by both. Certain bees make as many as one thousand stops along the way from food source to hive, leaving a well-marked scent trail that their fellows can follow.

Social bees, like termites, have highly organized societies but unlike termites they have no king. A typical colony of honey bees contains three castes. The largest is the worker caste, which consists of from twenty to sixty thousand nonreproductive females which perform most of the chores. They nurse, construct, defend and forage for food.

The second caste consists of several hundred males whose sole duty is to mate with the queen. They do no work and they have no stingers. Most of them are raised in late spring and early summer. In autumn, when the honey flow has ceased, the workers let the drones

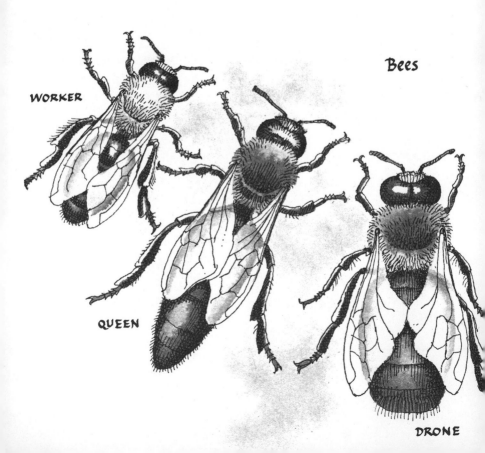

WORKER

Bees

QUEEN

DRONE

starve to death. The males no longer serve a useful purpose and feeding them would be wasteful when food is in short supply.

The third caste consists of the queen, a fully developed female that normally lays all of the eggs and is the mother of the entire colony.

The queen prevents any rivals from growing up by secreting a special scent substance from her jaw gland. This scent inhibits the development of the ovaries in the workers. It can also prevent ovary development in ants, flies and termites and, as if that weren't enough, it can kill mosquitoes and other insect invaders within the hive—a royal pesticide.

If the queen is removed from the hive, the workers' ovaries begin to grow. If she is put back, their ovaries shrink again. The queen substance is so powerful that it works even after her death. One researcher took a queen that had died three years before, cut her into pieces and placed the bits in the hive. The queen was, of course, unrecognizable as a monarch. Nevertheless, the hive workers' ovaries were affected just as if she had been alive.

Humans have long been intrigued by another bee-made substance, one which is fed to the queen. Newly hatched worker bees have head glands that secrete royal jelly, which, when fed to the queen, makes her grow large and keeps her that way.

Cosmetic manufacturers tried to sell royal jelly in face creams as a miracle ingredient which would keep women looking young, but it affects only queen bees.

The workers, in addition to feeding royal jelly to the queen, nourish the young larvae. Then, after a tour of duty as nurses, they become successively wax makers, house cleaners and air-conditioning operators (their wing flapping keeps things cool). It is only toward the end of their lives that they become honey gatherers for a few weeks. Finally, they wind up as guards.

Colonies containing healthy queens operate in a prescribed and efficient way. But if the queen is removed, things begin to happen. Workers become agitated and irritable. They fan their wings with a sound so loud that bee-keepers listen for it when seeking the queen in a divided hive. They know that the half with the loudest fanning does not contain the queen.

Under certain conditions, workers will react aggressively to the queen pheromone, killing the queen by stinging her or starving her. This happens when a mated queen is placed in a new colony or is removed from her own colony for several hours and then replaced. It can also happen when a second queen is inserted into a hive or when the bees are disturbed by too much handling.

Scientists consider the queen bee compound to be the most versatile pheromone yet discovered. It can function as an attractant for workers or for drones, as a swarming message and as a togetherness fragrance for colony cohesion. It can also serve as an alarm scent. When the temperature of the hive gets too high or when the queen is disturbed, the level of her scent rises and alerts the members of the hive to danger.

A change occurs when the number of bees in the hive begins to exceed fifty thousand or when the queen bee leaves the nest or becomes too feeble to continue her reproductive mission. It is theorized that an odor is released which causes the workers to select several larvae by some as yet unknown method. They do this within forty-eight hours after a queen is removed from a hive or dies or the population reaches the critical level. The potential queens, which are larvae less than three days old, are placed in specially constructed queen cells which look like half peanut shells. The young adult queens crawl out of the compartments when they are sixteen days old. If two or more queens emerge at once, they fight until only one remains alive. The surviving young queen then takes her first flight and is soon pursued by drones. Once she is fertilized, she can lay eggs for the rest of her lifetime of about five years, even if she never mates again. She can lay as many as two thousand eggs per year. Some of her eggs are unfertilized. These become drones and fertilized eggs become workers.

The new queen may return to the home hive after she mates. If the old queen is still there, the elderly monarch may leave with hundreds of workers in a swarm to find a new nest.

Evidently, the queen pheromone inhibits the raising of a new queen most of the time while the old queen is still vigorous.

One entomologist conducted an interesting experiment. He took a hive, removed all the young and left only the queen and some old workers. He took a second hive and moved it to a new location so that forager bees out in the field could not return to it. In the second hive, only the queen and the young bees were left at home.

In the first instance, where there were only the queen and the elderly bees, the queen continued to produce young and the old bees nursed them. But the glands of the old bees, which had atrophied, began to work again. The elderly insects were truly rejuvenated.

In the second case, where all the older bees were shut out, the development of a few young bees was speeded up. Their glands atrophied rapidly. In other words, they aged quickly, left the hive and began bringing back food to save the colony from starvation.

Most honey bees live in enclosed nests, for instance, dark cavities within hollow trees, crevices in rocks or boxlike structures provided by man. In these dark enclosures, the thousands of bees are crowded together and organization is achieved almost entirely by scent.

Worker bees are constantly sending and receiving messages. The enclosed nest offers protection from variable wind currents that could dissipate the scent signals. Nest enclosure, combined with active ventilation, also permits control over pheromone concentration. The fanning of wings sends inside air outside through vents in the nest so that scent messages do not remain after they have become meaningless.

Wing fanning also diffuses odor messages through the colony very quickly.

All debris within is carried outside and bees never eliminate wastes within the hive. Still, there is a unique smell of home. When a stock of bees is put into a hive, they show no hostility at first to strangers in their midst. They must reside in their new home for two or three days and create a home scent before they react aggressively to a stranger. The unique smell of the hive is probably derived from body metabolism as well as from the pollens and other plant products carried into the hive from many sources.

Each worker leaving the home hive for field duty carries a sample of home scent in a special sac. As she returns and alights on the sill of the hive, she opens the sac as though displaying an entry pass. Only bees with the proper hive odor are admitted.

On the other hand, a bee approaching a strange hive will suddenly veer away as if it smelled a repellent which said, "Stay out!"

What smells good to a bee, however, does not necessarily smell good to us. Bees quench their thirst in stagnant water. Among their favorite drinking spots are urinals.

Why do bees sting? They usually don't unless

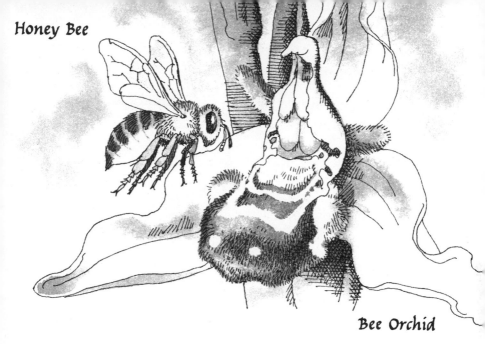

Honey Bee

Bee Orchid

threatened. Once one stings, however, the victim may be subjected to numerous and rapid stings. As long ago as 1814, scientists discovered that a fresh bee sting excited other bees. Bee keepers maintain that when there are multiple bee stings there is an odor reminiscent of sweet banana oil.

One plant that imitates a bee's smell is the orchid. The flower has a striking resemblance to the female bee in size, color and shape. A part of the flower even has hairs which look like those on the bee's belly. Male bees are attracted to the flower by the scent, which resembles the come-hither perfume of the female bee. When the male bees attempt to woo the flower, pollination takes place.

Another group of highly organized social insects which have long fascinated humans consists of ants. There are about six thousand different species, six hundred of which are found in the United States.

Most ant colonies have a single large queen which, as a winged virgin, left her mother's nest with a lone male for a nuptial flight. During the aerial courtship, the male transferred to the female all the sperm cells she would need for the rest of her lifetime—up to fifteen years. As soon as he performed his duty, the male died. The new queen, now minus her wings, set about establishing a colony for her offspring.

Ants, like termites and bees, have elaborate societies which consist mostly of workers. A worker ant may be a hunter, food gatherer, farmer or stock breeder, although in some species individual ants perform more than one of these roles.

The younger workers usually take care of the eggs, which turn into wormlike white larvae. The workers lick the larvae to keep them from getting moldy and put food into their mouths.

The larvae grow and change into pupae which still cannot move. When a pupa has developed into a young adult ready to hatch, the older ants help it to come out by tearing open the case around it.

The adult ants' devotion to the larvae is due to a sweetish liquid that the larvae secrete. The "nurses" evidently love the taste.

The young adult ants which are nurses have other jobs as well, such as cleaning the nest and building new rooms.

The older adult ants usually go outside to find food. The hunters among them generally have a stinger but some Indian species kill a beetle by pulling on its limbs in opposite directions. This may take an hour. The hunting party then drags the dead insect back to the nest.

Everything is cooperative in ant colonies. The American fire ant, for instance, may discover a dead butterfly which is too heavy for it to carry home alone, so it quickly runs to the colony to fetch help, marking the way back with a scent trail, just as Hansel and Gretel dropped breadcrumbs.

Ants mark trails with a scent gland called a gaster which makes a fine line of liquid. The odor rises into the air and can attract ants from both sides of the line at a distance of almost an inch.

Ants first head directly for the trail and then march single file, exactly along the marking, directly to the objective.

An ant of a different species, however, will not be attracted by the smell, but ant predators sometimes will. That's one of the reasons that the trail of a fire ant, for instance, evaporates within two minutes. Another reason is because it would be a disadvantage for the trail to last longer. If the quarry was eaten or carried off and the trail did not evaporate, thousands of ants would continue to head for it in vain.

If a source of food is abundant, paths will very quickly appear with markings constantly renewed by countless ants, scented intensively enough to cause a mass influx. As soon as the source of food is exhausted, the scent trail disappears, since ants which do not find food do not leave any scent arrows behind.

Ants also cooperate in battle, as they do in hunting for food. Researchers from the University of Connecticut observed an army ant colony in Ecuador. They watched as a single ant met an enemy wasp. Since the ant was only a third of an inch long, it was no match for the "giant" insect.

The single ant rushed back to a column of its fellow army ants and moved up and down the line touching antennae briefly with each ant. Within minutes, an assault force of hundreds was recruited and marching toward the enemy.

The scientists point out that the rapid recruitment methods of the army ant have obvious survival value because a small number of attacking ants would be more readily thrown out of nests by wasps than a large number. When ants in sufficient force attack, adult wasps abandon their nests, leaving their immature young behind to be devoured.

In the past, researchers thought that army ants, which got their name from the fact that they travel in huge columns, foraged blindly, eating whatever they stumbled upon. The researchers from Connecticut found, however, that the ants send out scouts to locate suitable food and lay down scent trails.

The dreaded African driver ants probably communicate as the army ants do. The driver ants feed on everything that does not flee in time, from aphids to pythons and, reportedly, unlucky humans. Driver ants send out a vanguard which sights the prey and then leaves a scent trail on the way back. The main army receives the information, advances, surrounds the victim and strips it to the bone.

Species of both bees and ants raid colonies of other social insects to obtain either food or immature workers that can be utilized as slaves. When raiding, they employ chemical warfare, emitting an alarm pheromone which sends the attacked colony into panic. The members then no longer cooperate and, thus, can't defend themselves.

Usually, ants use their own alarm scents to protect themselves. If only a single ant is attacked, there is not enough scent to alert the entire colony since the chemical is effective only over a distance of a half to two inches. However, when a number of colony members are attacked and the alarm scent is pervasive enough, the entire group becomes aroused to furious action. If they are inside the nest, they will attack. If they are outside, most will try to run away.

When a member is injured or dead, the other ants will nurse it, despite its smashed or twisted shape, until it begins to decay and smell. Then its fellows haul it off to the funeral grounds outside the nest.

When a Harvard professor perfumed live worker ants with the funeral pheromone, the scented ants were carried to the cemetery, although they put up valiant resistance. Once at the burial grounds, they hurried back to the

nest only to be carted off again thirty more times until the smell of death had worn off their bodies.

Scientists believe that ants have a vocabulary of at least ten pheromones and that by combining different ones or by changing the intensity or frequency of emission, they may be able to communicate scores of messages.

Just how much ants communicate and cooperate is obvious from the way they pass food around. Ants have two stomachs. The first, the crop, is a supermarket shopping cart in which they bring home the food supply to share with colleagues.

One researcher gave a single white transparent ant blue-colored honey. Within twenty-four hours, all the ants in the colony had the telltale blue honey showing through their bodies.

The ants use the second stomach to feed themselves. In one unique species, the honey pots, members of the colony act as storage bins. They gorge themselves on sugary liquids obtained from other insects and swell enormously. Then they hang from the ceilings of their underground homes. In times of scarcity, hungry ants nudge the hanging ants and receive food.

If ants are pests at picnics, cockroaches are

pests all the time. The cockroach is reputed to be the oldest insect on earth. It has survived for at least 300 million years.

Today, there are some five thousand species around the world, fifty-seven of which are found in the United States. Four, the American, Oriental, brown-banded and German roach live in every state.

The roach goes through three rapid stages in early life. The adult female drops her eggs anywhere at all, enclosed in protective capsules. She may drop as many as fifty-eight capsules at a time. In a few hours, the capsules split along a seam, exposing two rows of roaches facing each other. There may be twelve to forty roaches in each unit.

The baby roaches take a deep breath and the capsule opens. They emerge white and soft. Upon exposure to the air, their outer skins turn brown. At this point, they can live for about two weeks without food. From then on, it is a matter of growth. Approximately six to seven months are required to reach the adult stage from the egg stage. The entire life span for the roach may be two or three years.

The German roach seems to be prolific to the extreme. According to the National Pest Control Association, given ample food and moisture, a German roach can produce a family of up to 2 million offspring a year. In the typical breeding season, however, a single female averages about thirty-five thousand offspring.

Roaches like darkness and moisture, so leaky faucets, loose flooring and openings around pipes are favorite living places.

These pests eat almost anything—grease, cracker crumbs, bookbindings, postage stamps, soap and beer. They contaminate human food with germs such as typhoid and cholera and are generally offensive.

The mature male cockroaches are highly active and touch antennae with any other cockroach they meet. Should a male happen upon a female, she greets him by secreting a substance which really excites him. The male raises his wings and lowers his abdomen for as long as a minute. The female will then nibble at the secretion of the glands on the male's back. The secretion contains a substance, seducin, which makes the female keep still so the male can mate with her.

The male German cockroach has to receive the female's courting chemical by direct application—body to body—but the female come-hither chemical of the airborne American roach is a strong vapor.

Cockroaches of various species follow trails of feces pheromones and they also secrete a let's-get-together pheromone. Their aggregation chemical is nowhere near as spectacular in effect as that of the locusts, however.

One of the most amazing demonstrations of scent signaling occurs with those small grasshoppers. One day, they are solitary, hopping around and eating, and the next, they start turning into a destructive horde of locusts. This change is triggered by a powerful scent of togetherness. The pheromone works only over a distance of an inch or two. Nothing happens until a critical density of population has been reached. What causes the critical density is thought to be climate and the availability of food. The grasshoppers begin to multiply. The more that get together, the more fertile they become. The first generation represents a transition form. The reproductive avalanche continues. The second generation grows larger. The grandchildren no longer resemble their grandparents. Before they can fly, nymphs form into bands which seem to be gripped in a nervous desire for action.

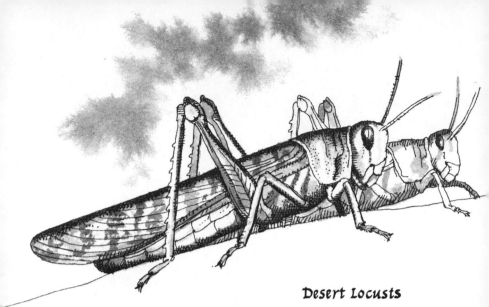

Desert Locusts

The separate bands keep gathering together to form a burgeoning army. The hopping of small groups spreads like a wave over the whole community. The dynamic rhythmic motions keep growing more and more excited.

The youthful army of migratory locusts, now in the billions and still unable to fly, begin to carry out a voracious march across the countryside, walking in a single direction, climbing over steep rocks. If they come to water or a crevice, the front column forms a living bridge so that the others can march over their bodies.

When the winged adult stage is reached, the

locust swarms take flight spontaneously on warm dry days when their body temperature reaches sufficient levels. The muscular activity of the flight raises their temperature higher and they can cease flying only when conditions change. Rain, a fall in temperature or the darkness of night will usually stop a flight, but the distances traveled may be tremendous. Swarms of locusts have been seen twelve hundred miles at sea. Their numbers may also be spectacular. One swarm sighted over the Red Sea in 1889 was estimated at two thousand square miles in size.

Once on the move, a locust swarm is almost impossible to stop completely. Destruction of eggs, digging of trenches to trap the nymphs, the use of hopperdozers to crush their bodies, and dusting with pesticides have all proved virtually ineffective. Fire doesn't work either. When farmers try to light fires to halt the invasion destroying their crops, the flames are smothered by the charred bodies of locusts and the rest of the insects march over them.

Locusts continue in a band until the swarm is finally destroyed by rain and cold. Once there is sufficient dispersement of the group, the scent of togetherness fades and the remaining locusts are again transformed into solitary grasshoppers.

While the grasshopper scent causes a population explosion, a pheromone produced by the flour beetle is a self-made contraceptive. If the beetle population rises above two beetles per gram of flour, the female begins to devour her eggs immediately after laying them. Why? Scientists have discovered that the beetle's waste contains a scent which has the cumulative effect of reducing the fertility of the entire population in a storehouse. It can prolong the time it takes for the larvae—called meal worms—to develop into beetles. As the concentration grows even stronger, it then triggers egg cannibalism.

Some pheromones are attractive to more than one insect. The almond meal moth and the Indian meal moth, which shared a common ancestor, produce the same pheromone. Interspecific mating does not produce viable offspring and therefore would lead to the eventual destruction of the species. This doesn't happen, however, because the females have a chemical which turns off the wrong mate. The female almond meal moth repels an Indian meal moth with a "stink bomb."

Females of many insect species exercise careful control in choosing mates. A male fruit-fly, for instance, will approach a prospective mate and vibrate his wings. If she has already mated, is of a different species or is too immature, she sends out a stink which rejects him.

The female's turn-down of the wrong male protects the species. Theoretically, males can mate with more than one female and have little to lose beyond some reproductive cells. But an error in mating is serious for the female. Once her eggs are fertilized, she cannot increase her offspring by mating a second time. The wrong mate could cause her to lose the entire season's, perhaps her entire lifetime's, potential offspring.

Another way things are kept straight when insect come-hither chemicals are similar is through the timing of signals. The grain weevil, for instance, will emit her come-hither scent from 11 P.M. to 4 A.M., while a close weevil relative will emit her scent from 2 A.M. to 6 A.M..

The female silkworm and other insects have one type of molecule in their come-hither perfume which reacts to a specific spot on their male's antennae. This makes it possible for the two appropriate insects to get together despite the billions of scents in the air at one time.

There is little room for error in the selection of a mate. The silkworm moth, for instance, lives only on air during its brief adult life and is incapable of absorbing food or drink. Therefore, it has a very small amount of energy to fulfill its function as a mate. The male must conserve his strength and can't fly around looking for a likely female. He sits and waits until the wind blows a few female scent molecules onto his antennae and then makes directly for the target.

The approach of a potential mate, particularly among flying insects, is a complex sequence of behaviors. It includes the initiation of flight, directed movement, stopping and landing. The control of these events may involve various types of mechanisms but they are thought to be largely regulated by pheromones and by visual stimuli.

The principal female response to male-produced sex pheromones appears to be either inhibition of the female's natural tendency to fly or cessation of flight.

A male butterfly, for instance, is attracted to a female flying overhead. He soars into the air to overtake the female and then distributes a special scent over her which induces her to land.

A male moth, on the other hand, uses a scent to prevent the female from taking flight.

Learning more about insect pheromones will be of great benefit to humans. Pheromones do not kill pests but they can be used to lure unwanted insects into traps where they can be killed. And unlike current pesticides, pheromones are not harmful to other creatures. Pheromones can also be used to saturate the air and confuse insects so that they are unable to find mates and are therefore unable to reproduce. Or pheromones can be used to inhibit the mating response of some insects. Scientists at the U. S. Department of Agriculture found that if the pheromone of the lesser peach tree borer is mixed with the pheromone of the peach tree borer, the mating response of both insects is inhibited.

By using pheromones to lure insects, humans would be imitating certain plants which produce odors that attract insects for pollination purposes. One may give off the odor of dead meat to lure flies while another uses the sweet smell of flowers to attract bees.

Humans themselves are unfortunately attractive to certain insects, but some of us are more attractive than others. It is believed that mosquitoes respond to the lactic acid in our sweat and breath and to the carbon dioxide we exhale. People differ in their metabolisms; some of us put out more lactic acid and carbon dioxide than others and are therefore more likely to be bitten. In fact, we, as individuals, may be more attractive at one time than at another.

It is only the female mosquito which bites. Male mosquitoes are vegetarians, living solely on plant juices. The females need additional protein to mature their eggs and they obtain it by drinking animal blood.

Those who do not wish to be stung by bees are advised not to look or smell like a flower. That means, bright clothing and perfumes, including hair sprays, should be avoided when you're in bees' territory.

Bees and other insects often recognize their food by sniffing it out. Once they find it, they may need further chemical stimulants to induce them to bite into the plant tissue and, finally, they may need yet another chemical cue to make them swallow. Through this elaborate mechanism, an insect is protected from ingesting plant material which might be harmful to it.

The power of insect scent-detecting ability is no more evident than in the ichneumon fly and Ephialtes wasp.

In one experiment, a scientist took the cocoon

of a moth to an area in which the ichneumon fly had never been seen before. When the scientist opened the moth cocoon in the woods, a scent arose from it. Within fifteen minutes, a whole swarm of ichneumon females appeared and settled not only on the cocoon but also on the experimenter's hands, where moth scent remained.

Female ichneumons can hunt out victims hidden deep in tree trunks. They put their eggs

Ichneumon Fly

only into other insects such as caterpillars, spiders and queen ants. It is believed the fly either hears or smells the host deep in the wood, then pushes its ovipositor, or egg-laying device, three inches into the tree. The ichneumon usually hits right on target.

When male ichneumons await females breaking out of the wood, they listen for drilling sounds. Sometimes, they are fooled into waiting for a beetle or some other insect that sounds like the female fly. Not only do the ichneumons have to make sure they don't try to mate with a beetle, they have to be sure they don't mate with a female belonging to two closely related species of flies. Therefore, the males feel and smell the emerging insect with their long antennae to find out if she is the right one.

The Ephialtes wasp, like the ichneumon fly, deposits its young in the body of a living creature. Most of the time, the mother chooses the larva of some other insect. Flitting from one cabbage to another all day long, the mother may find the caterpillar of the cabbage butterfly, or she may find some larvae concealed deep in wood, for instance those of the wood wasp. But unlike the ichneumon fly, the Ephialtes doesn't use sounds to help her find a likely host; she relies on smell alone. When the wasp finally finds the right spot, it raises its abdomen, places its needle-sharp egg depositor against the bark of a tree and drills a hole right through to the hapless host.

Ephialtes wasps like to eat the beetle *Tenebrio molitor,* which hides itself so well in grain silos that the only way to find it is by smelling it out. Not only can the wasp sniff out its beetle prey, it can tell by scent whether the beetle has reached a suitable stage of development. A pupal caterpillar, which the wasp does not eat, is not attacked.

Insects can even be used as bloodhounds. There is the story of an old plumber who was called in when no one could find the source of a terrible stink in a factory. The stench was so bad that the unions refused to work.

The plumber arrived with a container of blue bottle flies which he had just captured in a butcher shop. He opened the lid of the jar and allowed the insects to escape. He watched as they settled on a small area of the factory wall. He walked over, made a hole at the spot where the flies were and found an open drain which had been covered up years before. The flies had accomplished what human investigators could not.

V
A Bird with a Beak Doesn't Smell Very Well

A hawk soars high in the sky and suddenly divebombs to the earth below to scoop up a small rabbit or a snake.

A vulture sits patiently on a tree branch waiting for a dying animal to be still.

Does the hawk or the vulture use scent to find food? Can birds smell?

Birds are very visible and very vocal animals. Virtually all communicate with others of their own species and with other birds and with mammals, including us. They usually do so by means of sound or by visual signals such as color or elaborate movements.

There are from ten to twelve thousand species of birds. They come in all varieties but they share one thing in common, feathers.

Their closest relatives, strange as it may seem, are the reptiles, but unlike reptiles, which depend heavily on the sense of smell,

Black Vulture

birds rely more on sight and hearing to gather information from the environment. Birds have acute hearing and super sight.

The sense of smell would not be of much benefit to the hawk, for instance, as it flies high in the sky or covers great distances.

The vulture, on the other hand, has a well-developed sense of smell. In the mid-1960s, scientists demonstrated in the laboratory that it reacts to different odors with changes in respiration and pulse rate. But when other scientists covered carrion, the vulture's favorite meal, with a cloth, vultures flying in the sky did not find it, despite the strong odor of decay.

Observers believe that when vultures are perched on any tall point in their habitat—a treetop or mountain—and one of them sees carrion lying on the ground, they all follow the movements of the first bird swooping down on the prize. Smell has nothing to do with it.

Or has it? Vultures are voiceless. Do they

Kiwi

only communicate with visual signals? No one knows yet.

Zoologists, at first, believed that perhaps the flightless kiwi birds of New Zealand were the only birds that used scent rather than sight to locate food. The nostrils of the nocturnal kiwi, unlike those of other birds, are near the tip of its bill.

There are many shapes and sizes of beaks, which serve as feeding tubes, organs of touch and receptors for vibrations. The beaks or bills do have holes which look very much like nostrils. And, in 1911, scientists reported that birds have the necessary olfactory structures. They have an olfactory bulb in their brains and nerves that carry impulses to the hindbrain. Still, there was doubt that birds used these structures to smell. Then, in 1963, Professor Walter Neuhaus of Erlangen University in Germany showed that pigeons and turkey vultures can react to different odors. He noted, however, that seedeaters have little need for an olfactory sense compared to species which live on green plants.

Five years later, other scientists reported that the brain areas receiving smell messages are largest in swimming birds, intermediate in marsh birds and small in all others. This, they said, suggests that most water birds, marsh dwellers and waders and possibly some other species have a useful sense of smell, but that in all other species, it is probably unimportant.

Is smell really unimportant for birds or is its use among them as yet undiscovered?

The fact that most birds are gregarious—they like to be together—is significant. In all other gregarious creatures, smell plays an important part in their societies. What brings birds together into a flock? Is it only the sight of similar beings?

Farmers have long told of the pecking order of chickens. The most superior one pecks the one below it and that one pecks the next lowest and so forth. The pecking order can be affected by injections of hormones. Pheromone and hormone production are interrelated in animal groups other than birds, and dominance is signaled by scent in fish, rabbits, dogs and many other animals. Could the pecking order of chickens be affected by odors?

Although it is not yet known whether birds use smells to communicate, it is known that they have a scent which can be detected by predators. Quail and other ground-nesting birds build their nests without lining, not, according to experts, because the ground-nesters are less skilled than other birds but because this makes it easy for the earth to absorb their scent and therefore helps protect them from predators. They lay their eggs, then keep their feathers tight around their bodies while fluffing them around the eggs or toward the soil.

The real "stinker" among birds is the mountain blackbird of Eurasia, also called the ring ouzel and Turdus Torquatus. Despite its beautiful clear piping song, farmers and gamekeepers of Eurasia and Northern Europe hate the bird because its strong smell distracts their dogs from their work.

Some researchers believe that it is possible that birds use their body odors to signal since, among some species, when nests are built close to one another, breeding seems to be stimulated. Is this due to the sight of other birds or is it due to smell, as it is among other animals?

The question of whether or not the sense of smell plays an important role in the lives of birds remains, as yet, unanswered.

VI
Rodents, Rabbits and Other Small Mammals

When a group of female mice live with males, the sexual cycle of the females is synchronized. They are all ready or not ready for mating at the same time. If a new one is placed in the colony, she soon joins in the rhythm.

Should a newly pregnant female mouse be exposed to a male from a strange colony, she loses her unborn baby and is then ready for mating with the stranger.

The synchronization of the female mice cycle is called the Whitten Effect, for W. K. Whitten of the Jackson Laboratory, Bar Harbor, Maine, who first described the phenomenon in 1956. He observed that when no males were present, the female cycles became irregular. When males were present, all the females reached estrus at the same time. Therefore, mating readiness could be affected by the addition or removal of males.

Dr. Whitten further concluded that the regulation of the female cycle was controlled by an odor substance in male urine.

The pregnancy block is called the Bruce Effect, for Dr. Hilda Bruce of the Department of Investigative Medicine at Cambridge, England, who first reported it. She discovered that if a pregnant female was exposed to a new male within three days after mating, she lost her fetus.

Both the Whitten Effect and the Bruce Effect are controlled by odors. This has been proved by researchers who blocked the sense of smell in female mice. When the females could not smell the male odors, their hormones were not affected. Neither the synchrony of their estrous cycles nor the loss of their fetuses took place.

The behavior of rats, mice, rabbits, hamsters, gerbils, skunks and hundreds of other small mammals is spectacularly controlled by such scent messages. The animals literally converse with urine, feces and with the products of special smell glands.

Odors affect every aspect of their lives, and with good reason. In a world where visibility is limited by the tops of blades of grass, and where it may be safe to move around only at night, the sense of smell can provide information about the environment, family, friends and enemies.

Rodents are the largest order of mammals both in number of individuals and in the number of species. They are distinguished by their jaws and teeth, which are uniquely adapted for gnawing. The majority of rodents are small or medium-sized. To describe them as numerous is an understatement. In any large city, the rats alone probably equal or outnumber the humans.

Odors provide powerful warning signals to rats. Scientists first observed the freezing behavior of these rodents in the presence of a cat in 1920. The rats remained stationary for three to thirty minutes when a cat was placed nearby. During that time, the rats did not eat, care for their young, sleep or mate. However, when the cat was enclosed in a sealed glass container or the rats' nostrils were plugged so they could not smell, the rodents went about their business without the slightest alarm.

In more recent experiments, investigators discovered that the outcome of scientific projects involving rats and learning may be affected by human odors. In one laboratory, rats were divided between two caretakers, each of whom provided all maintenance for his own animals, including handling once a week for eleven weeks. The rats were then tested to see which side of an open field activity box they preferred. An open field activity box is an enclosed box which is divided into smaller, semienclosed areas. The animal can run freely about from area to area. Play objects and the caretakers were systematically moved about the test space.

The results were that the rats spent significantly more time on the side where their own caretaker was stationed when they could smell him. The rats handled by the experimenter who

Desert Woodrats

had worn the same unlaundered sweatshirt for the entire experiment showed a stronger preference than those handled by the experimenter who had worn a clean shirt every day.

In the laboratory or in the wild, odor messages play a vital role in both the sex life and parental behavior of rodents.

Scientists have observed that on or near the date when wild females are capable of conception, the behavior of both sexes changes. The female rats wander more than usual beyond the limits of their customary home range, actively looking for males.

When a female finds a male, she touches noses with him and then each inspects the other's genital region. The female then moves away. After following her for a few feet, the male returns to his own activity. But the female doesn't give up. She wanders about the place, rubbing her sexy scent against fences or in burrows, on trees or on posts. She drags her genital-anal region over the soil, leaving a scent trail. The male is finally smitten and repeats her path-marking performance until he locates her in a burrow. He then rubs and rolls and drags his body around the burrow entrance to erect a scent sign for other males which says, "Stay away. She's mine."

Researchers at the University of Pennsylvania have closely observed the courtship behavior of house mice. The experimenters have discovered that mice use urine and/or perputial (penis) gland odors in courtship.

Urination is a convenient means of sex identification for mice. It does not require close and perhaps dangerous contact. Male urine and penis odor causes aggressive reactions among strange males, and a male will urinate much less in the presence of strange males than in the presence of strange females. In addition, the urine of dominant males contains an odor which discourages subordinate males from trespassing in their territory.

Compared to males, females deposit very little urine in the presence of strangers, but female mouse urine has its own special powers. In addition to identifying a mouse as a female, it contains a tranquilizer so that she can pass through male territory without being attacked. Scientists have found that when they rub a male mouse with female urine and place him among strange males who would normally attack him, the scented male is treated as gently as a female mouse.

Copious male urination in the presence of females serves to synchronize female "heat" cycles and induces earlier maturation of young females. The compounds in the male urine which affect female hormones are probably pheromones produced by male hormones. When males are castrated, the smell of their urine no longer has an effect on females. But if they are castrated and then given male hormone replacement, their urine is once again potent.

Sexual behavior in rats and mice does not depend entirely upon olfaction. Females who have lost their ability to smell continue to cycle and to mate. Odors do play a major role, however, in the selection of a mate and in the female's readiness to mate. This is probably truer in the wild than in captivity.

Certain other rodents depend almost entirely upon the sense of smell to find a partner and to become parents. Hamsters which have had the smell portion of their brains removed no longer show mating behavior. Gerbils, small rodents often kept as pets, show loss of maternal behavior when their olfactory bulbs are removed from their brains.

Parental behavior in most rodents is profoundly affected by odors. For instance, if a female mouse loses her sense of smell before she has her first litter, she kills her pups. A female who is an experienced mother and loses her sense of smell does not kill her new pups but may have trouble determining which are hers and which are another mother's.

This has led researchers to believe that there is a family odor by which mothers can recognize their own offspring and, conversely, by which their own offspring can recognize them.

The odor of the mother rat will inhibit the activity of her infants at first, keeping them near and quiet so they will not be in danger from predators. Then, from about the fourteenth day after birth until the twenty-seventh, the lactating mother rats produce a strong maternal scent that pups can smell at a distance. This allows them to wander off to explore and yet enables them to follow their noses back home.

Scientists are certain that olfactory cues received by infant rats and mice immediately after birth contribute to their memories of familiar smells. Such odors forever signify "home" and "family." But these odor messages have been found to have far more effect on female babies than on males.

When lactating rat mothers were injected with a smelly substance, citral, which then contaminated their milk, the female offspring formed a stronger preference for the citral odor than the males.

When experimenters put perfume on parents, the female mice pups grew up to prefer mates who were perfumed with the same scent. Again, the males were not as strongly affected.

Female mice pups are also more affected by the presence or absence of a father than males. Females reared only by their mothers were indifferent to males in adulthood. Furthermore, female mice exposed to males in babyhood reached sexual maturity at an earlier age than females not exposed to males.

Perhaps female mice are more affected by family smells than males because they are the ones who choose mates and who care for the young. Nevertheless, males are affected more than females by some scent signals. The males use scent to determine who's boss within an area.

If you've had a pet hamster or mouse, you know that after you've carefully cleaned their cage, it smells again in no time at all. The rodents intensify the production of their personal odors by increasing defecation and urination in clean or strange places. They soon ensure that their environment is permeated with their own odor. In fact, they even build odor fences.

Most species of small mammals mark territories. A rabbit marks boundaries with a chin gland; a vole squirts a secretion on its paws and then stamps out its property line.

A territory is a "defended region." Within such a space, an individual, pair or group of animals lives peacefully. Strangers trying to enter are repulsed.

Almost all species of animals that display territorial behavior are, to some extent, gregarious. They like to be with others of their kind.

We humans began to worry about population density and birth control only recently but animals have set their own numbers per area since the beginning of time. If healthy young are to be raised, the family must be in a safe, uncrowded place with enough to eat. Animals use odor as a lasting signpost which lets others know their territory is taken even when they are away from home. A potential intruder can smell another's area at a distance and therefore avoid the danger of treading upon someone else's property. As Robert Frost, the poet, said, "Good fences make good neighbors."

Humans have territories, too. Amazonian Indians, for instance, put skulls on sticks to designate their boundaries and anyone entering within does so at the risk of life and limb. While most of us don't go to such extremes, we do mark our properties with picket fences or we pile up stones to show where our land begins and ends.

Rodent families mark out territories in warehouses, larders and cellars. Boundaries are marked with lumps of feces. If the mice are not disturbed by rats, cats or men, their constant marking with urine and feces creates pillars which reach a height of up to two inches and look like stalagmites in a cave.

As mentioned before, mature male house mice are viciously attacked if they venture too far into another male's territory. Once defeated by a superior male, the subordinate one will cower when exposed to the winner's scent.

The amount of male hormone decreases in the urine of defeated males, thus changing the strength of their territory message when they urinate.

The dominance system and marking behavior may be affected by the degree of crowding, however. When territorial defenses break down, one male may become dominant in all

Mongolian Gerbil

available territories. A hierarchy is formed with only the superior one marking. Nearly all his marking is done in newly acquired areas.

In one study of gerbils, the dominant male marked an average of 23.1 times in 30 minutes in a new territory while he marked only 3.8 times in 30 minutes in his home territory.

Nondominant animals are still capable of marking but they simply do not when in a dominated territory. If a defeated male is moved to a new area, however, his scent marking behavior returns to prebout levels. However, if he is placed in a new area soiled with sawdust and feces from the dominated territory he just left, he does not renew marking.

While almost all small mammals mark, they do not all use the same method.

Among gerbils, for instance, both the males and the females deposit a pheromone by rubbing an abdominal scent gland on objects and on each other. The male marks to show dominance, to signpost a territory and to leave a "calling card" when exploring. The female marks when exploring and when claiming pups. She retrieves pups and marks them, regardless of whose they are. Both sexes mark more during nest building and their aggressive tendencies increase during parenthood.

A hamster male marks frequently when placed in an empty cage belonging to another hamster of either sex in an attempt to show potential dominance. He marks less frequently in his own cage.

The amount of marking a male hamster does in a cage belonging to a female varies according to the day of her estrous cycle. If she is ready for mating, he marks very little, perhaps because of a special tranquilizer she emits.

A female hamster marks much more when placed in an empty cage belonging to another female than she does if the cage belongs to a male. Some females mark hardly at all in a male's cage.

Lemurs are less subtle. These monkeylike animals found in Madagascar hold stink fights. When marking with scented palms or tails doesn't work to warn off rivals, males will raise their tails and shoot smells at each other for as long as an hour.

But one of the clearest societal uses of scents is that of rabbits. There is a striking correlation between a high rate of marking and a high social status.

Rabbits live in small social groups, each occupying a territory. There is a hierarchy among the males of the area and among the females. A dominant male and female rule the group.

Rabbits have two scent glands which are used to mark for social dominance and territoriality. They deposit the secretion of one, the chin gland, by a form of marking called "chinning." Dominant males chin more frequently than subordinate males and dominant females chin more than subordinate females.

Rabbits deposit the secretion of the other gland, their anal gland, with their feces. Anal markings of dominant rabbits are frequently either larger or more smelly. Rabbits scatter unmarked feces about but they pile up marked feces at prominent locations in their territory as signposts.

In another interesting use of scent, dominant rabbits will raise their tails as a sign of victory. This presumably allows their full anal scent to escape. Defeated rabbits will press their tails down tightly, much as scared dogs do to hide their scent.

Both the chin and the anal glands are larger and heavier in dominant males.

No one is sure why some animals such as rabbits mark with more than one source of scent. Are they sending different messages or are they transmitting the same message in different ways? If the message is the same, perhaps one scent might be more likely to survive under humid conditions while another might be better in dry conditions.

Rabbits vary from many other small mammals in that the males are ready to copulate all year long, provided females are anywhere around. There is no need for physical or visual contact to attract the males. The smell of the female is enough.

The male rabbit will mark his chosen female with urine. The female will then carry his personal ownership scent around with her.

Rabbits' societies are very cohesive. In fact, researchers noted that in one experiment where wild rabbits were crowded together in a pen, the caged rabbits did not try to escape but individual rabbits stranded outside tried to force their way in.

The scent of society membership, of course, affects rabbit parental behavior. Females confronted in their own pens with young of other members, their own young and completely strange offspring, treated them all differently. They tolerated their own progeny, harassed those born to other females of the colony but viciously attacked and killed almost all the strange young ones.

All small mammals seem to emit a special fear odor just as sea creatures emit an alarm chemical. Many experiments have demonstrated that mice prefer the odor of unstressed mice to that of mice who have been subjected to stress.

Rats that were taught to press bars for various rewards showed a dramatic loss of ability to perform when the odor of rats in pain was wafted into their cages.

Responses to the fear and pain of others may be learned. Mice raised in isolation past weaning were all capable of eliciting the alarm or fear response in other rodents but they, themselves, did not respond to fear odors emanating from others. The ability to respond appears to develop between three and five weeks of age. Mice isolated at five weeks were able to show aversion to the odors of stressed animals. Mice regrouped for fifteen weeks after early social isolation developed some responsiveness to the fear scent but did not show the highly significant responses of normally reared mice.

The selection of food by rats is also odor-related. It has been demonstrated that a sudden removal of an odorous material which had been added to the food causes a temporary overeating. This fact suggests to scientists that smell cues are involved in effectively limiting the daily intake of rodents to a suitable calorie level.

There are still many mysteries about how small mammals talk with scent but there is one small mammal whose use of scent is well known.

The skunk's use of smell as a defensive weapon is scent talk at its loudest.

A skunk gives an enemy fair warning by arching its back and opening its mouth in a threatening manner. The skunk lowers its head, growls and stares directly at its foe. The striped, bushy-tailed mammal then stamps the ground with its forefeet or rakes at the grass with its long claws. One type of skunk, the spotted, adds to its threat display by standing on its front paws, advancing against its foe with its hindquarters and tail elevated.

Finally, if the enemy still does not back down, the skunk archs its tail over its back, turns its body sideways in a U shape and spews out a

Scent Gland

SCENT SAC   RECTUM

ANUS   TAIL

Striped Skunk

pungent spray of musk from a pair of anal scent glands.

The skunk's glands produce about one-third of a liquid ounce of amber-colored musk, about enough for five consecutive discharges.

So accurate is the animal with its spray that it can reach the eyes of an enemy from a distance of up to thirteen feet. The liquid can burn and cause temporary blindness. The smell, however, is the most potent weapon. It is nauseating and lasting. It may even cause vomiting.

Skunks have long used this scent, but only as a last-resort defensive weapon. They never use it against their own kind. But humans have employed it against their own kind. During World War I, the U. S. Army used skunk odor to mask poison gas. Later, they used the skunk odor alone to fool the enemy. The Germans had learned to associate the scent with the gas, so as soon as they smelled skunk, they hurried to put on their gas masks and to beat a hasty retreat. The Americans, on the other hand, unfettered by the cumbersome gas masks, advanced on the enemy without a problem.

VII
On the Trail with Dogs and Cats

A nine-year-old girl was missing from a small town in Massachusetts. She had gone to the store for some candy about 8 P.M. and then disappeared from earth, as if a space ship had swooped down and scooped her up.

State Police Trooper Robert Heck had a less romantic idea. He believed the little girl had met with foul play and he suspected her stepfather.

He was right about the foul play but wrong about the stepfather.

A trainer of bloodhounds at the time, Trooper Heck has since been promoted. He is now a police specialist with the United States Department of Justice, and is in charge of the training programs for police dogs used in airport security. But he remembers the case of the little girl as if it happened a few days ago.

Any dog can distinguish human perspiration

diluted to as much as one part per million. The smell sensory area in the canine's nasal passages is about the size of a handkerchief compared to our dime-sized area. But just as some people have a better sense of smell than others, so do some dogs.

The flat-nosed Pekingese and the English bulldog have a comparatively poor olfactory capacity. The German shepherd has a smell capacity at least forty-four times better than ours but the bloodhound has the best sense of smell of all breeds. The shepherd can follow a smell trail eight inches wide but a bloodhound's track extends to three and a half feet.

We humans sweat on the palms of our hands and on the soles of our feet in response to stress or exercise (but not to heat). This form of sweating is believed to be part of our instinctive reaction to danger. The moisture enables us to run faster or grip better because it creates more friction. It's the same thing as licking your thumb before you turn a page or spitting in your palm to obtain a better hold on a ball.

Criminals under the stress of trying to escape capture sweat profusely on their palms and soles and therefore leave a smellier trail than usual.

People who are lost, on the other hand, are more difficult to track because when they begin their journey they are not under stress. They do not know they are about to become lost.

Nevertheless, when anyone, criminal, lost child or you, walks barefoot over the ground, about four-billionths of a gram of odorous sweat is lost per step. Even with shoes on, billions of odor molecules in sweat are being pressed through to the ground. Neither rubber nor leather can prevent the depositing of a trail.

No two people smell exactly alike, not even identical twins. Shepherds and bloodhounds can crisscross the tracks of many people and pick out a specific individual's trail from among the others.

An important advantage that such dogs have over humans is that their noses don't get "tired" as quickly. You know that if you walk into a room, no matter how strong an odor may be, within a few minutes you won't smell it anymore. But a bloodhound does not become "blind" to a scent for more than 39 hours.

Furthermore, Trooper Heck reports, bloodhounds can follow trails that are up to 109 hours old. They can also track a person from a piece of wood, even though the person washed his or her

hands before touching it and then handled it for only a few seconds.

However, Trooper Heck said, bloodhounds have some disadvantages. They're messy because they slobber a lot, they can't see well and they aren't very good at protecting their masters. In fact, when he used a bloodhound to track down criminals, he had to tie the dog to a tree to get it out of the way before making the actual capture.

That's why law enforcement officers prefer to work with German shepherds which, while not as good at tracking as bloodhounds, give better protection and are more pleasant to have around.

Getting back to the missing little girl. The bloodhound used in the case was given an item of the child's clothing to sniff. That's called "firing up the hound for the track." Then the dog was taken to the place where the youngster was last seen, in front of the candy store.

The dog sniffed and sniffed and led the police to a candy wrapper. It then walked around to the curb as if looking for a parked car. After that the animal headed back around behind the candy store.

Trooper Heck explained that bloodhounds

have an amazing ability to follow a scent in sequence. If a person goes off the road and detours but comes back within ten minutes, the dog will stay on the road. But if the person stays off the road more than ten minutes, the dog will follow the detour and then return to the original trail.

The bloodhound in the case of the missing girl returned to the street from behind the store and then trotted off down the road as if following a car. It kept going until it came to a bridge where there was a grating. A dog can follow a human scent which leaks through a car—the older the car, the more the leakage. Unfortunately, the strong winds over the bridge's grating had carried off the scent and the trail ended there.

But the dog had led the police to believe the girl had gotten into a car. Neighbors, indeed, remembered that a green car was parked at the curb the night the child disappeared.

In the meantime, the police went through their files and found a card on a known child molester who lived in the area. They checked, and sure enough, he owned a green car.

When the man was confronted by the dog, which found the scent of the girl in the car, he confessed. The killer said he had told the girl that he had a puppy and the girl could walk it. The child asked to see the dog. The man told her he'd meet her behind the store with the puppy. There he dragged her into his car and killed her. Her body was found in a gravel pit eight miles away, a few miles beyond the bridge.

Bloodhounds were originally an English breed but Trooper Heck said that the British hound has been so overbred that it is now a lazy monster. It weighs about 145 pounds. He said that it is so heavy it would have little stamina if it had to track for any distance.

The American bloodhound today is much sleeker, probably because it was interbred with southern coonhounds sometime in the 1800s.

Bloodhounds use their nose more than their eyes. They can catch a scent which has drifted up from the ground and is several feet in the air. They have the most trouble tracking in sunlight because the sun's heat makes the scent oils and molecules rise eight or nine feet and attach to trees. But in the coolness of the evening, the scent molecules drop to the ground and tracking is easier than on a hot sunny day.

Another problem in tracking can occur when a missing person is from a home where there is a tendency to exchange clothing. Trooper Heck gave as an example the case of a missing teenaged girl. The police officer in charge of the dog knew that the girl customarily exchanged clothes, including bathrobes, with her sisters and that the sisters all slept in the same room.

The officer asked the family members to line up. Each time he gave the dog the scent of the clothes most recently worn by the missing girl, the dog went to the family line-up and sniffed. Each time the dog picked a member who had also worn the garment, the officer said "No" and refired the scent. Finally, the dog realized that it was supposed to track the scent which was not from a person in the line-up.

Prisoners, well aware of this phenomenon, will try to fool the dog tracking an escapee by placing other people's shoes and clothes in the escapee's cell.

Trooper Heck said that he knew inmates did this so he always asked to go to the place where entering prisoners placed their personal belongings. Trooper Heck would then select the escapee's wallet or keys or some other item that would retain personal scent indefinitely.

The police specialist related many tales of the bloodhound's fantastic tracking ability. He told of one case in which an elderly couple's car was stolen and used in a robbery. The man had used the car for years. Since most of the human scent in a car comes from the anal gland, it would have been useless to have the dog sniff the car seat. The elderly man had used the car for so long that his scent would have overpowered any new odor.

Instead, the dog was directed to sniff the wheel of the car. The dog picked up the new scent and followed it a mile and a half down the road, where three robbers were found hiding.

In another case, a couple had been picnicking and were robbed. The two felons warned them not to move or to call the police. To make sure that they couldn't be followed by car, the robbers yanked the spark plug wires and threw them into the woods, where the police officers found them.

A dog was brought in, sniffed the wires and successfully picked up the trail of the robbers.

In still another case, a bank holdup man spit out his gum during the excitement of the crime. Since it is highly unlikely that anyone would touch someone else's gum, a bloodhound was brought in, sniffed the gum and followed the scent to a construction company where workers reported they had seen two men get into a car. Two weeks later, a car of the same description was used in another robbery and, this time, someone wrote down the license plate number and the robbers were captured. One of them liked to chew gum.

Because they do not make good pets and because there are few who wish to undertake their training, American bloodhounds are in short supply. Israelis use them to track Arab infiltrators who try to sneak across the border but requests for the dogs far outstrip their availability. A mercenary who wanted to buy American hounds to track Mau Mau terrorists infiltrating into Southern Rhodesia a number of years ago, could not get them.

In growing supply, however, is the next best canine smeller, the German shepherd. Shepherds have been used in the United States since the early 1960s to sniff out narcotics and bombs.

The use of dogs to sniff out narcotics is not that new. The British Imperial Troops in Alexandria, Egypt, employed dogs in the 1870s to find hashish being illegally smuggled out of the port.

The police specialist reported that most

German shepherds being used are trained at Lackland Air Force Base under a grant from the Law Enforcement Assistance Administration (LEAA), an arm of the U. S. Justice Department. The handlers trained there are members of local police agencies from all over the United States.

Graduates of the training program are located at thirty airports. They search warehouses, cars, lobbies and baggage rooms. The dogs are trained under a variety of weather conditions and aboard all types of aircraft.

Dogs are also used at shipping ports and other places where contraband may be smuggled in. It is not necessary that containers be opened. The animals can smell the illegal material even if it is packed in tin or steel. The scent leaks through microscopically small holes.

The dogs are trained for twenty-one weeks for patrol and bomb detection duties. After training, they are tested every six months. Explosives are hidden and then there is a wait of forty-five minutes. If the dogs cannot pick up the scent within fifteen minutes, the test is considered a failure and they are either retrained or retired from the program.

The average time it takes a dog to cover an

entire airport for explosives is about thirty-two minutes and the average locker area can be gone over in less than seven minutes. Of course any dog can have a bad day, and if the handler is in a bad mood, it may throw the dog off the scent.

Mr. Heck thinks that beagles, which are small relatives of bloodhounds, might actually be even better than either the hound or the shepherd. He reported that one law enforcement officer hand-held a trained beagle like a vacuum cleaner. The officer would raise and lower the dog along curtains and bookshelves in the search for contraband. The dog was excellent at turning up loot.

A trained pig would probably be even better at smelling than a dog but can you picture a policeman walking a pig on a leash?

The giant St. Bernard rescue dogs are famous. They can find a person trapped beneath an avalanche and tell whether someone caught under huge snowdrifts is alive or dead. The heavily furred dogs can defy blizzards and dig rapidly at the burial spot of a luckless skier. But the Swiss are now using German shepherds instead of St. Bernards because they are easier to handle and just as good at smelling out buried humans.

In Holland, a variety of dogs are trained for sniffing out gas leaks. The animals are taught to stay at the spot where they detect gas and to bark. Although the broken gas pipe may be far underneath the pavement, the dog's nose is more sensitive than most modern equipment and the dogs are more portable.

There have even been suggestions in medical journals that dogs be employed in diagnosis. Dogs have a great memory for scents. If they could be trained to detect abnormal products in blood, sweat, urine and plasma known to be excreted in different disorders, then they would be better than any machine now in use and much cheaper.

A hotel in Africa, plagued by burglaries, used a dog for diagnosis of a different kind. A traveler reported that he arrived at the hotel and, while checking in, noticed that a huge Newfoundland dog came from behind the counter and sniffed his luggage.

The traveler thought nothing of it and went to the bar to have a few drinks before going to his room. After the drinks, however, he was a little foggy and couldn't quite remember his room number. He started off in the wrong direction and the Newfoundland jumped in front of him and barked and growled. The man turned back and the dog calmly followed him.

The traveler suddenly recalled his room number. When he opened the door to enter, the dog squeezed in front of him and went directly to his luggage. The dog sniffed the bags, sniffed the traveler and then trotted out of the room wagging his tail.

Needless to say, there had been no robberies in the hotel while the dog was in residence.

Burglars sometimes fool male guard dogs by rubbing themselves with the scent of a female dog. This immediately calms the canine protector, and puts it off guard.

It is still not clear just how much information is exchanged by scent between dogs. Everyone has seen both male and female dogs sniffing at each other's rear parts but what message are they receiving?

Male dogs are also often observed leaving scent marks at fire hydrants, lampposts, trees and, in fact, anything upright and straight.

The dog's wild relative, the wolf, also marks with urine. It establishes scent stations around stumps, sticks and logs.

Scientists studying wolves observed that on a wide open expanse such as a frozen lake any

Wolf

conspicuous object may become a scent signpost. Sometimes several wolves of a pack will
wait in line to urinate at the same place. They
may repeat this routine each time they pass by
until a large amount of frozen urine accumu-
lates over the winter.

According to the researchers, the scent posts
provide information on the number and size of
social units and it is obvious from the behavior
of wolves that these message drops have some
meaning to other wolves outside the pack.

What message does a pet dog receive when it sniffs a lamppost where another dog has urinated? According to researchers, a male sniffer will react in one of three ways. He will scratch the ground vigorously with his hind legs and growl because he has smelled the mark of another male, one which he believes is a potential rival.

Or he will whine after more sniffing and trot away, which means that he has recognized the scent of a female.

But if the dog trots away without either whining or growling and scratching, he considers the mark unimportant, probably that of a smaller or at least an inferior male.

Dogs, when they approach each other directly, also give and receive messages. Two canines may near each other until they are within sniffing distance. Then they will hold their tails upright and their ears flat and they may issue deep-throated growls as they slowly circle each other.

One dog may wag his tail as a sign of dominance, not friendliness. Probably what he is actually doing is fanning his scent toward the potential rival.

The dogs may then go their separate ways or they may curl their upper lips, electing to fight. If one dog doesn't want to battle, he puts his tail between his legs to hide his scent and may cower or run.

When a dog gives up in battle or does not wish to fight when attacked, it exposes a vulnerable part of its body, such as its throat, to the opponent. The victor honors this act of submission by ceasing the attack and then urinates on the closest post as a sign of triumph.

There is much yet to learn about dogs and scent messages, even though dogs have been domesticated for so long. However, a study of their close relative, the fox, may provide more information. Observers have found that the red fox hatches sea gull eggs. It gathers them soon after they are laid by gulls. Since the gull's eggs are easy prey, the fox can gather much more than it can eat or carry, so it buries the surplus in the sand.

The fox has a reputation for being clever, but the fact is that its wiles come as much from its keen senses of smell, hearing and sight as from intelligence. The fox can't quite remember where it buried its booty, so it must find it again by using its nose.

The fox can pinpoint the exact location of sea gull eggs it buried four inches deep in the ground if it passes within three yards of the buried eggs.

Young rabbits, which foxes also like, are protected from their enemy because foxes are "blind" to their scent. When left buried in sand by their mother while she searches for food, the young rabbits are almost always missed by a prowling fox.

Humans and domestic canines have established a fast friendship through the centuries. Dogs have been employed to hunt, guard, gather and track. They have even been used as substitute eyes for the blind and noses for those with poor olfactory powers.

The dog even recognizes changes in the odor of its human friends.

The fact that dogs can determine moods has been observed by anyone who has ever owned a dog. In fact, Trooper Heck said that his bloodhounds could tell from a distance of 250 yards whether someone approaching was friendly toward him, a sufficient distance to allow him to ready his defenses.

A dog which is separated from its beloved master may die of grief. There is a story told about an Irishwoman who landed with her dog at an English port. Since the British will not allow dogs into the country without a period of quarantine, the woman could not take her dog with her. As the custom official placed the dog in a basket, the woman slipped off her shoe and put it in the basket too. She knew that her pet would grieve and she was willing to limp away to the train with one shoe on and one shoe off so that her dog could be comforted while she complied with the law.

If you've ever owned both a dog and a cat or observed them for even the briefest time with their masters, you know the differences in their behavior. A dog is typically a friendly, communicative animal, eager for an exchange of information between itself and humans and others of its own kind.

Cats may also be friendly and very fond of their masters, but they are basically loners. They are far less communicative.

A dog uses sounds, motions and scents to give messages. Cats use these methods also, but to a lesser extent.

The differences in behavior and communication go back to the animals' wild ancestors. Dogs and their relatives usually hunt in packs and share food and shelter. They form societies in which there is a dominant leader. Through years of domestication, the dog has transferred its allegiance from the pack leader to its human master. And because there is competition and cooperation among pack animals, the dog has a great need to communicate.

Cats, on the other hand, with the exception of the lion, hunt alone or in small groups. The mother cat and her young are generally the only social unit.

Self-reliant and independent, the cats nonetheless heavily employ their sense of smell. They often hunt at night when smell is more useful than sight. The smell sensory area in their nasal passages is relatively larger than that of several breeds of dogs and is proportionally about twice the size of humans'.

The cat's sense of smell is crucial to its eating habits, and when its nasal passages have been clogged due to disease the cat often loses its appetite completely.

Cats deposit scent marks just as dogs do. The marks represent road signs. A fresh mark may denote "Detour, this section taken." A less fresh one may mean "Proceed with caution" and an old mark may signify it is all right to walk through the territory.

Such signposts are made with urine. They serve the purpose of keeping potential rivals for mates and for food from meeting.

There is no fixed breeding season among cats.

The estrus or heat of a female lasts about a week and recurs every three weeks. The felines use scent to pick prospective partners.

Female cats, according to some researchers, also have a special scent which is specifically designed to get rid of a male suitor when she's had enough and wants him to get lost.

We humans, of course, have used the cat to protect us from rodents as well as to provide companionship and affection.

We have also used the smell produced by a

Civet

certain type of cat, the civet, which is found in Africa and Asia. The perineal glands of both the male and female civet cat open under the tail into a large pouch which collects greasy, musk-like secretions. The civets use the substance to mark out territories on trees, stones and other posts. They are solitary and hunt at night. The smelly material is also used to seek a mate.

Because the civet cat's smell substance makes its message last for so long on its sign-posts, humans have obtained it and used it in commerce. It is put in human perfumes to make the fragrance linger.

VIII
The Prime Sense
Among the Primates

The primates are an order of mammals which includes the primitive tree shrews of Southeast Asia, the lemurs of Madagascar, the monkeys and apes of Africa and us.

The word *primate* comes from the Latin *prima sedes* meaning "first see" or "the highest rank." The animals in the order are considered to be the most advanced on earth.

In prehuman times, of all the sense organs, the nose was probably the most important for survival. It gathered information at a distance about food, prospective mates and danger. But when primates took to the trees, their snouts or muzzles flattened so that their eyes could see better. In the treetops, vision, especially depth perception, becomes most important. If you are swinging through trees, it helps if both eyes can focus on the same object.

Along with the shrinking snout in primates,

there were changes in the brain. There was a progressive increase in the size of the organ with an accompanying enlargement of the skull to hold it. But there was a reduction in the brain area which receives smell messages.

In mammals such as rodents and carnivores that depend almost entirely on olfaction for survival, the smell areas of the brain are relatively large. But in monkeys, apes and humans there is a marked reduction of all olfactory equipment.

However, despite the fact that primates are considered microsomatic, or less powerful smellers than the dog or the moth, they still have tremendous olfactory capabilities. Smell messages, of course, are most useful to the primates that feed at night and are constantly in danger from predators. But all primates, including humans, converse with scent signals to some extent.

Prosimians, the most primitive primates such as the tree shrews, have skins supplied with sweat and sebaceous glands which function as message producers. The tree shrew, for instance, uses glands on the throat and chest areas to mark out territory. The lemur employs glands located on its forearm and armpit. It may

Cross Section of Human Brain

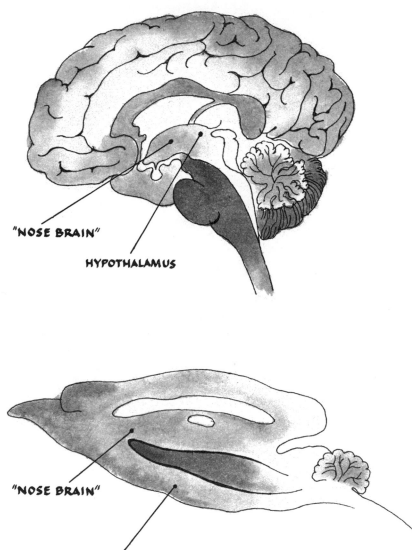

"NOSE BRAIN"

HYPOTHALAMUS

"NOSE BRAIN"

HYPOTHALAMUS

Cross Section of Rat Brain

run its forearm directly on vegetation to leave a trail or it may first rub the end of its tail on the forearm gland and then use its tail as a perfume stick. The bush baby spreads urine on its hands and feet and then stamps out a scent border around its territory. Many prosimians mark their mates to show ownership.

Until very recently, scientists believed there was no odor communication among the higher primates. Now, it has been discovered that a great deal of information is communicated by scents, some of it, among humans, subconsciously.

Many higher primate males are strongly attracted to the scents of females in heat.

Spider monkey females, for instance, do not show any visual signs of cycling, so that scent cues are the only means of transmitting sexual information.

Scientists have stimulated the production of scent signals in some primate females by treating them with the female hormone, estrogen. Adult rhesus monkeys under free-ranging conditions, living on an island off the coast of Puerto Rico, breed seasonally. But when experimenters implanted the females with estrogen pellets, the females became sexually receptive at any time of the year, and as a result of the signals from the treated females, male rhesus monkeys showed not only sexual interest but hormonal readiness to mate. This means that the presence of estrogen in the female rhesus can induce changes not only in her but in the glandular function and behavior of the male with whom she interacts. This effect is undoubtedly produced by smell.

The conjecture that scent signals are at work was borne out by researchers in India who conducted thorough studies of a troop of bonnet monkeys, six adult females and four adult males. When one of the females came into heat, three males mated with her. That the signal was carried by odor seemed to be proven by the behavior of the fourth male in the troop. He was diseased, blind and incapable of mating. Yet, when in the vicinity of the female in heat, he was drawn to her. He could only have been aware of her by scent.

Volatile chemicals secreted by sexually ready female monkeys were actually isolated in the early 1970s by Dr. Richard Michael, formerly of Britain and now at Emory University in Georgia. He named them copulin. He isolated almost the identical compounds from fertile

Female Gorilla

Male Gorilla

Rhesus Monkey

women. He and his co-workers were able to link peak production of the secretions to the times of ovulation in women.

The level of secretions was significantly lower in women who were taking birth control pills than in those who were not. This suggested to the investigators that the birth control pills in some way interfere with the production of the compounds.

Dr. Michael believes that his work demonstrates that the same odor substances which act as sex pheromones in nonhuman primates occur as normal constituents of the vaginal secretions in women. The role of olfaction in human sexual behavior is unclear but there is research that suggests it has a function in our own species. Many researchers are still reluctant, however, to identify a substance as a human pheromone.

Most other mammals produce scent substances with apocrines, which are modified oil glands. Ordinary oil or sebaceous glands emit a fatty substance which keeps hair and skin lubricated. Eccrine glands secrete sweat to regulate body temperature. The apocrines secrete a scented liquid.

The hair under humans' arms and around their genitals serves to collect the odor of the apocrine glands' scented liquid. In humans, as in other mammals, the apocrines are small and hair is sparse around the genitals until growth is stimulated by hormones at the time of puberty.

Whites, blacks and Orientals differ in body odors because they have a different distribution of these specialized scent glands. Blacks and whites have numerous apocrines under the arms, in the genital region and on the chest. Blacks have more than whites but the most striking difference is in Orientals, who have little body hair and a sparse distribution of apocrine glands. The Japanese have more apocrines than the Chinese but far fewer than whites and blacks. In fact, in Japan, if a man has underarm odor—caused by bacteria working on the secretions of the eccrines and apocrines—he can obtain a medical excuse from serving in the armed forces.

The Koreans hardly have to worry about body odor at all. They are almost devoid of apocrines and give off very little scent, even when careless about hygiene.

Smell certainly plays a part in the form of human communication known as "kissing." This was recognized in the Bible when Jacob tricked the blind Isaac into bestowing on him the divine blessing meant for Esau. Isaac first asked Jacob to kiss him. Isaac's intention was to identify his son Esau by smell, but the father's nose was fooled because Jacob wore his brother's clothes.

Since the nose is directly over the mouth, we smell what we kiss. In some cultures people are direct about it and greet each other with a sniff. Eskimos, Maoris, Samoans and Philippine Islanders rub noses or place their mouths and noses against the cheek of another person and inhale as a means of identification. In some of their languages, the word for kissing means "smelling" and Borneans never "greet" anyone, they "smell" them.

When Arabs talk to each other, they stand very close so they can get a whiff of each other's breath. To deny another one's breath is considered an insult. It is also an Arab custom for a man's family to smell a girl before she is selected for his bride.

The English language, too, has long recognized the importance of smell in social behavior. What do we call people who are so mean and untrustworthy that they should be avoided? Stinkers!

How do we refer to people who think they are

better than everyone else? We call them "snobs" or say they are "snooty." They literally or figuratively stick their noses up in the air to avoid the smell of people they consider inferior to themselves.

Like most creatures on earth, humans accept or avoid others partly on the basis of how they smell. No matter how we scrub and clean ourselves, we all smell. It is not just a matter of the scents produced by apocrines but of odors resulting from what we eat, what we use and where we live.

Trained perfumers or "noses" can detect by scent what you have eaten for the past two days and they can determine a great deal about your life-style and the ethnic group to which you belong. They can also tell, of course, what fragrance you are wearing, providing that you sprinkled yourself with it sometime within the past several hours. Your body metabolism can change the odor of perfume and it can also affect the other scents you give off.

Many odors are identifiable even to an untrained "nose" who may or may not be conscious of what he or she is smelling. Central Europeans, for instance, carry the scent of the cabbage, turnips and radishes in their diet while

Indians smell of rice and spices and South Sea Islanders of fruit and palm. Americans smell like butter to the Japanese, who in turn smell like fish to Americans. To the rest of the world, Eskimos have the odor of blubber, oil and sweat.

How we smell to others matters a great deal to us. Sigmund Freud, the father of modern psychiatry, believed that our modern self-consciousness about how we smell and our subsequent repression of our awareness of odors was among the causes of mental illness.

Some social scientists today believe that one of the reasons the human sense of smell is not as sharp as it could be is because of the change from breast-feeding to bottle-feeding. They reason that frustration of the infant's instinctive search for the aromatic breast which has been replaced by the odorless bottle might inhibit the normal development of pleasurable reactions to healthy body odors. This theory received some support when a young California researcher, Michael Russell of the University of California Medical Center, discovered that nursing infants could, by the age of six weeks, distinguish their mothers' odors from those of other women.

It has also been suggested that repression of our ability to smell might cause the dramatic loss of odor-detecting ability seen at certain ages. It has been shown repeatedly in experiments that there is a very sharp drop in a child's ability to detect odors at about the age of ten years, coinciding with the beginning of social awareness and conformity. There is another drop in odor-detecting ability at the age of eighteen, the age of entrance into adulthood.

Capitalizing on our self-consciousness about our own odors and those of others, advertisers constantly tell us that we have bad breath and body odor and that we need products to correct these conditions. We spend billions on products to deodorize and reodorize ourselves and our homes.

And because sweet smells are pleasurable, manufacturers are leading us around by our noses. Only 20 percent of the fragrances produced annually are used in toiletries such as perfumes, aftershave lotions and bath products. The rest are used in everything from laundry detergents and furniture polishes to deodorants for glue factories. A leather scent, for instance, is added to plastic shoes to help sales and a "jaguar smell" is made for Chevrolets and other less expensive automobiles. There is even a "new car scent" for used cars.

To make ourselves smell more attractive, we

have long borrowed the products of the scent glands of animals. Ambergris is formed in the intestines of the sperm whale. Musk comes from a small gland near the sex organs of the male musk deer or from the muskrat; civet is the musky substance produced by the civet cat; and castor, a glandular secretion of the beaver. Such animal products are mainly used as fixatives to make our fragrances last longer.

Most of the musk being promoted so highly today is manufactured in the laboratory. There is a good reason for this. Hunting expeditions have to be organized to seek new supplies of animal scents. The elusive musk deer of the northern Himalayas browses at the snow line of the Tibetan mountains and moves mostly at night. Its musk can only be obtained when it is killed. The substance is then carried by caravan through China and India to the Burmese border. Civet from Abyssinia passes through many hands before it arrives at a London perfumery depot as an unattractive brown, greasy mass still packed in the hollow horn of a zebu, the humped domestic ox of northeast Africa.

So you see, humans will go to great lengths to obtain products that will make them smell better. In fact, if Spain hadn't been seeking perfumes and spices from India to make food and wealthy people smell better, America might not have been discovered by Columbus. He was looking for a new route to bring these products back to Europe.

We use animal scents to cover our own animal scent. And while musk from the musk ox in a perfume may make a human male feel romantic, scientists have found that the natural scent from a human female intrigues bulls, male goats and male monkeys. There are even stories of perfumed women being pursued by antlered bucks and by male beavers.

There is no doubt about it. Smells, both good and bad, play a part in human communication. But unfortunately, we make ourselves "deaf" to many of the messages, and fail to appreciate the wonder of this important sense.

We can only taste four things—salt, bitter, sour and sweet. Therefore, most of our enjoyment of food comes from its aroma, not its taste. Furthermore, our noses, directly over our mouths, constantly monitor every bite we take to make sure the food is not rotten.

When we sleep, our noses remain on guard, sampling the air for dangerous fumes. If smoke or another potentially harmful vapor is in the air, our noses usually wake us.

There are still many mysteries about the

sense of smell, not the least of which is how it works. How do we know that we are smelling a rose or vanilla within a fraction of a second after odor molecules reach our noses? How can we remember thousands of odors and identify something we've smelled only once when we smell it again years later? Are there primary odors just as there are primary colors?

The answers to these questions are still only guesses. But one thing is certain: odors can affect us both mentally and physically. Just think how we react when we smell something delicious. We smile and take a deep breath. And if something stinks, we wrinkle our noses and try not to breathe.

By becoming more aware of the wondrous information provided by smells, we can understand more about scent talk among animals—all animals. We can then gain a better understanding and greater enjoyment of the world in which we all live and smell.

Suggestions for Further Reading

Bedrick, Roy. *The Sense of Smell.* New York: Doubleday & Co., 1960.

Bellamy, David. *The Life-Giving Sea.* New York: Crown Publishers, 1975.

Birch, Martin, ed. *Pheromones.* Amsterdam, London: North-Holland Publishing Co., 1974.

Buchsbaum, Ralph. *Animals Without Backbones.* Chicago: Chicago Books, 1948.

Dennis, Felix, ed. *Man-Eating Sharks.* Secaucus, N. J.: Castle Books, 1976.

Droscher, Vitus B. *The Magic of the Senses.* New York: E. P. Dutton & Co., 1969.

Erb, Russell C. *The Common Scents of Smell.* Cleveland: World Publishing Co., 1968.

Evans, William F. *Communication in the Animal World.* New York: Thomas Y. Crowell Company, 1968.

Exploring Your Sense of Smell. U. S. Department of Agriculture Science Study Aids developed by John Boeschen, February 1975.

Genders, Roy. *Perfume Through the Ages.* New York: G. P. Putnam's Sons, 1972.

"Jaws—The Real Thing," *Time,* July 23, 1975.

Selsam, Millicent. *Ants.* New York: Four Winds Press, 1967.

Verrill, A. Hyatt. *Perfumes and Spices.* Boston: L. C. Page Co., 1940.

Index

RUTH WINTER, former science editor for the *Newark Star-Ledger*, is the widely read science columnist for the *Los Angeles Times* syndicate. The author of several books and numerous magazine articles on health and medicine, she lives with her husband, a neurosurgeon, and their three children in Short Hills, New Jersey.

RICHARD CUFFARI is a well-known artist whose work has won him numerous honors and awards. He has illustrated more than one hundred and thirty books for children.